Clinical Applications of Psychoanalytic Theory

Clinical Applications of Psychoanalytic Theory

Esther Fine, PhD

JASON ARONSON
Lanham • Boulder • New York • Toronto • Plymouth, UK

Published by Jason Aronson
A wholly owned subsidiary of The Rowman & Littlefield Publishing Group, Inc.
4501 Forbes Boulevard, Suite 200, Lanham, Maryland 20706
www.rowman.com

10 Thornbury Road, Plymouth PL6 7PP, United Kingdom

British Library Cataloguing in Publication Information Available

Library of Congress Cataloging-in-Publication Data

Fine, Esther, 1926–
Clinical applications of psychoanalytic theory / Esther Fine.
pages cm
Includes bibliographical references and index.
ISBN 978-0-7657-0949-3 (cloth : alk. paper) — ISBN 978-0-7657-0950-9 (electronic)
1. Psychoanalysis. I. Title.
RC509.F56 2012
616.89'17—dc23
2012051557

∞™ The paper used in this publication meets the minimum requirements of American National Standard for Information Sciences Permanence of Paper for Printed Library Materials, ANSI/NISO Z39.48-1992.

Printed in the United States of America

Contents

Prologue

In recent years there has been a burgeoning of theory construction in psychoanalysis and it has been accompanied by changes in therapeutic technique that have deviated from the traditional classical treatment model. My husband, Sidney Fine,[1] and I selected four different analytic schools of thought to examine: Classical, Self-psychological or Kohutian, Kleinian, and Kernbegian. At the outset of our endeavor, we were well aware that many more existed, and indeed there has even been a splintering within these four groups that has led to new forms of conceptual thinking and technical intervention since we began our study in 1980. I will review some of those deviations in this prologue. Nonetheless, I maintain that the ones chosen for this review represent a proper sampling of the sources of predominant approaches in psychoanalysis in the United States today.

We set out to examine the crucial similarities and differences among these groups in both theory and practice; more specifically we wished to determine whether and in what way the professed theoretical formulations were translated into interpretive interventions in an analytic session. These issues will be explored in the forthcoming chapters. My husband and I also coauthored the chapter on autism. In this opening section I want to take a closer look at the interconnection of theory and practice in psychoanalysis, to reflect on whether theoretical differences, even if translated into varying technical approaches, can be considered significant. Some maintain it is not (Wallerstein, 1990). I also want to address the issue of eclecticism, to respond to a current trend to encourage a blending of different points of view in accordance with what seems right to a given practitioner (Modell, 1994). Finally, I will briefly review recent theoretical and clinical offshoots from their respective classical analytic, Kleinian, and self-psychological roots.

The Interconnection between Theory and Practice

Theory in psychoanalysis is restricted by its subject manner; it deals primarily with subjective mental phenomena and must necessarily rely on hypothetical constructs to explain observable events. The very fact that the practice of psychoanalysis is dependent on inferred meanings of a patient's expressed mental representations necessitates working within a theoretical frame at the same time that it invites the creation of alternative explanatory concepts. The ideal theoretical construct, according to Loewald, "structures, thus always exemplifies, a complex aggregation of events, brings some order into an at-first chaotic constellation and sequence of events; it functions as an organizing principle which is gradually distilled out of the events when investigated in a certain perspective" (p. 66). However, every way of seeing (i.e., theorizing) can be a way of not seeing, so that a given theoretical focus may well blind the clinician to recognizing and understanding certain mental phenomena, in the process of highlighting others.

In examining the common ground shared by practicing psychoanalysts, particularly as it pertains to the analysis of the transference, Wallerstein (1990) has maintained that theoretical differences among analysts fade in their significance in the consulting room. It will be the theme of this book to examine such a position. To quote Weinshel (p. 85), "if it is indeed true that the transference neurosis is the central conceptual and technical vehicle of psychoanalysis as a therapy, then it is also true that whatever alters our concepts of the development, handling and resolution of that transference neurosis must simultaneously alter our very concept of what psychoanalysis is." As our research project (see chapter 2) demonstrated, transference and transference neurosis are indeed viewed differently in each of the theoretical schools under study.

Eclecticism: The question arises as to how to consider these multiple models of the human psyche and their respective treatment approaches. Is it possible to integrate the four theories into one? Certainly each body of theory has made its special contribution to understanding psychological development. Classical psychoanalytic theory has probably provided the broadest, most inclusive framework; whereas Kohut has deepened our understanding of the narcissistic personality, its development, and its treatment, especially in highlighting the importance in relating to the patient exclusively through his subjectivity. He has significantly helped us to focus more on concepts like empathy and introspection. The Kleinians have certainly increased our knowledge and understanding of the primitive dark side of man's nature . . . his greed, envy, and destructive impulses, and magnified our awareness of the primitive mechanisms of defense. Kernberg has broadened our understanding of object relations with his conceptualization of contradictory ego states, brought about by two opposing sets of self and object representation.

These conceptual differences will be examined more fully in the ensuing chapters; but now I will consider some issues involved in an eclectic approach, and the possibility of incurring logical and contradictory inconsistencies in such random selection. Mutually exclusive concepts cannot coexist within a single theory. While this issue will be addressed later in greater detail, it will suffice now to provide one example as it pertains to technique.

Each theoretical position demands that we use a special technique in the treatment of the patient. The classical technique encourages the development of a transference neurosis in which there is a delay in interpretation until transferences are clear and well formed. Interpreting the negative transferences as they arise is also important in the classical technique. Kleinians, on the other hand, believe that there is a full transference development on the first day of treatment, and deep interpretations can be given at the beginning of treatment. The self-psychologists take a different point of view. They feel that a long time is required for a transference to develop before interpretations can be offered; moreover, they encourage the development of an idealizing and mirroring self-object transference, they do not analyze conflict, and they do not interpret the negative transference, which has high priority in the classical, Kernbergian, and Kleinian schools. Such variation in the theory of technique underscores the hazards involved in eclecticism, which can lead to disjointed theoretical speculation and treatment approach.

If one wishes to mix and match theoretical ideas from the different schools, it behooves the individual to carefully learn the different languages used by these schools of thought. Ego in Kleinian theory differs from the classical concept of ego. Kernberg, in his blending of ego psychology and object relations, casts a somewhat different perspective on the same construct. Lastly, Kohut's concept of the self cannot be equated with any of the foregoing formulations of the concept of ego. By the same token, different theoretical terminology can signify the same or at least similar conceptualizations. These issues will be further elaborated in the chapters to follow; at this juncture one example will be presented. There is a parallel between the Kleinian concept of projective identification and the Kohutian concept of self-object. In each there is an internalization of an important object over which one needs to exert control. The forerunner of this process is contained in the classical Freudian concept of object cathexis and in the defense mechanism of projection. Kernberg (1955b), in an attempt to understand regression and identification in countertransference, proposes the concept of ego identity defined as a "precipitant of identifications involving very early object relationships" (p. 44), and proposes that projective identification is its primary archaic defense mechanism.

Both Kernberg and Kohut have proposed differing approaches to the treatment of narcissistically disordered individuals. Is there some relationship between the empathy so crucial in Kohut's theoretical formulations and the primitive empathy described by Kernberg? Or do their definitions of empathy on the part of the analyst differ so significantly that there is no basis for comparison? Such questions sound a cautionary note calling for careful scrutiny, and signaling the dangers of crosshatching theories. Nevertheless, such an attempt will be made in chapter 3. Chapters 1, 2, and 3 also provide a description of the analytic perspectives under study—how they differ and how they are similar. Chapters 4 through 9 provide case examples of the application of psychoanalytic theory, and the final chapter, 10, summarizes current theories of therapeutic action. I hope that this prologue has prepared the reader for the chapters that follow. Before concluding this introduction, I also wish to express my appreciation to my analytic friends and colleagues who have contributed to the book's form and content: Gerald Aronson, MD; Alfred Goldberg, MD; Elyn Saks, JD, PhD; Janet Smith, PhD; and my daughter. Lisa Fine MD

CHAPTER DESCRIPTIONS

Chapter 1: Three Theoretical Perspectives on Child Development. In this chapter three psychoanalytic languages will be examined with specific reference to their attempt to explain child development in both normal and deviant forms. Concepts they hold in common will be described as well as significant differences. How differences in theoretical orientation affect clinical intervention in treatment will also be discussed.

Chapter 2: Four Psychoanalytic Perspectives. This chapter describes a research study which examines two hypotheses: 1) there are detectable differences in interpretive style among classical, Kleinian, Kohutian, and Kernbergian analysts; and 2) the nature of these differences can be discerned and described. Statistical findings are presented, along with clinical examples, followed by a discussion of their implications.

Chapter 3: The Protective Devices of the Human Psyche. This chapter describes the defensive strategies of four psychoanalytic perspectives, classical, Kleinian, Kernbergian, and self-psychological, focusing on the similarities and differences among these schools as it relates to their defensive constellations. The possibility of crossing theoretical boundaries to build a more comprehensive picture of psychic defenses is discussed.

Chapter 4: Latency. It is the period that signals a halt to infantile sexuality, although the latency phase need not bring about an interruption of sexual interest, as the case example that is presented suggests.

Chapter 5: Guidelines for a Positive Therapeutic Outcome. The chapter reviews the goals of the classical psychoanalytic process, illustrated by the clinical case of a six-year-old boy in psychoanalytically oriented psychotherapy.

Chapter 6: From Autism to Oedipus. The chapter first provides a historical perspective of the study and treatment of autism. Varying approaches are cited—neurobiochemical and hematologic studies and studies connecting autism to an organic brain disorder. Psychoanalytic views of the disorder are discussed. A case example of the successful treatment of an autistic child is presented.

Chapter 7: ADHD. The chapter reviews the controversy regarding the etiology of ADHD—those who favor a neurological explanation and treat with medication and those who focus on the psychological underpinnings of the disorder and prefer a psychotherapeutic approach. The case of a seven-year-old boy with an ADHD diagnosis is presented. He had been treated with Ritalin and it had not been helpful. His successful psychotherapeutic experience is described.

Chapter 8: Grapes of Wrath. The chapter examines the common elements in the psychology of physically abused children. Two clinical cases are presented: a nine-year-old girl, suffering from a school phobia, and a twelve-year-old girl with suicidal ideation. A tripartite model is suggested to account for the underlying similarities in their psychodynamics.

Chapter 9: The Psychodynamics of Physical and Sexual Child Abuse. In this chapter, the dynamics of the abusive parent as well as the abused child are presented, including a case example.

Chapter 10: New Age in Psychoanalysis. The focus in the last chapter is on current views of the effectiveness of psychoanalytic treatment. Therapeutic action is a relatively new term in the psychoanalytic language that refers to how the analyst tries to achieve a positive treatment outcome. The views of different analytic perspectives are presented.

NOTE

1. Sidney Fine, MD: psychoanalyst, died June 25, 1985.

Chapter One

Three Theoretical Perspectives on Child Development

Since its inception psychoanalysis has provided a forum for divergent views. Its loosely woven theoretical framework facilitated the introduction of a wide range of theoretical formulations on psychic phenomena, some contradictory and inconsistent with others, and some providing linkages in building blocks for more systematic theory construction. The vicissitudes of psychoanalytic theorizing had led to the establishment of different schools of thought, different analytic perspectives, and each has evolved theoretical perspectives that attempt to explain child development, both in its normal and deviant forms. An effort will be made to ferret out concepts in common among the three theories presented in this chapter that may be obscured by the use of different terminology, as well as examine the real differences sometimes obscured by similarities of language. Each theoretical group has evolved its own schema and timetable for child development, along with explanations for normality and pathology: an attempt will be made to clarify these differences. The question of how differences in theoretical orientation influence clinical or technical intervention in treatment will also be examined as well as the question of whether it is possible to have a unitary theory of development which would encompass the best of each theoretical perspective.

The three theoretical perspectives to be examined will be referred to as: 1) Classical, 2) Kleinian, and 3) Self-psychological, or Kohutian. These labels are shortcut terms to designate clusters of theoretical ideas. Of course it is not possible to do justice to the fullness and complexity of each body of theory, nor can I completely account for the wide range of contradictory ideas I found within each group. This review will undoubtedly seem an oversimplification in many instances: but, it will demarcate the key concepts in each body of theory, provide some linking concepts that underlie the theories' distinguishing features and demonstrate ways in which each theory applies its concepts in clinical practice.

First it would be well to have a definition of child development that all perspectives would accept. The likelihood is that all would agree that child development involves a process of growth in which there is a progressive differentiation and integration of the parts that make up the whole. More specifically, there is an expectable progressive sequence in the evolvement of the child's psychic apparatus and reasons why there might be deviation from the normal progression toward maturation.

It is likely that the three theoretical groups under study would probably agree with the broad general definition of child development that I have just cited, although the self-psychology group, and possibly the Kleinian group, might prefer the term self rather than psychic apparatus. Classical Freudian theory has always had a developmental orientation. In recent years, however, there has been an increasing focus on the ongoing forward-looking developmental processes, an interest that stems primarily from direct observation studies in contrast to the more traditional method of gathering data, namely through a reconstructive analysis. A fundamental concept in the developmentalist schema is that human development is a continuing and lifelong process. Moreover, psychoanalytic treatment is viewed in and of itself as involving a developmental process. Proponents of the developmentalist point of view include Calvin Settlage, Virginia Clower, and Morton Shane. Their conceptual guidelines are drawn from the work of Margaret Mahler and Anna Freud, as well as their clinical work with children. However, their basic conceptualizations about child development rest on the foundations of classical analytic theory.

Essentially, there have been three periods of classical analytic theory-building. The first period is mainly concerned with the libido theory and the role of sexual and aggressive instinctual drives. The libido theory is based on the assumption that the sources of the sexual instinct stem from somatic processes, biological in nature, which, in turn, pressure the psychic apparatus. Freud postulated a sequence of libidinal phases: from oral to anal to phallic and oedipal, then latency, puberty, adolescence, followed by a mature genital phase. The concepts of regression and fixation are essential ones in this phase-centered psychology. Although the period of the libido theory was succeeded by two other periods, the concept of the libido has remained as an essential component of classical psychoanalytic theory and practice. It does not assume such importance in the other two theories to be discussed. In fact, the self-psychological school has dismissed the libido theory as a viable conceptualization.

The second period of theory-building in classical psychoanalysis has been termed the era of ego psychology. It heralded Freud's structural theory: the division of the psychic apparatus into three agencies—the id, ego, and the superego. The term ego has been used in all three theories, but it assumes different meaning in each theory. In classical analytic theory, the ego stands for the executive apparatus of the psyche, engaged in its task of regulating the id, superego, and the adaptation to external reality. It is the seat of perception, memory, affect, and thought. It was hypothesized that there was a struggle among the three agencies of the mind, and indeed within the ego itself, which could pose a threat to the harmonious functioning of the total mental system. As with the libido theory, the conflict-derived psychology became a controversial issue and a point from which the two other theories we will consider chose to deviate, particularly self-psychology.

The third and most recent period of theory-building has been primarily concerned with the role of the earliest object relationships. It has been concerned with the developmental processes of separation-individuation, and this object relations psychology has ushered in a new dictionary of theoretical terminology. The term object was introduced very early in psychoanalytic theory to stand for the loved person. The initial term Freud used to examine the sexual drive, in fact, was the sexual object, the person to whom the individual felt sexually attracted. Object came to be the word to designate the significant other in a person's life. There is controversy in the schemas of the different theoretical models as to when a relationship with a significant other begins. Is an object relation formed at birth, or are there transitional steps before that can be achieved?

Object constancy is a central concept in psychoanalytic developmental theory and refers to the individual's capacity to distinguish between objects and to maintain a relationship to one specific object, regardless of whether his needs are being satisfied. When object constancy has been achieved, the child is capable of maintaining a positive image of the absent mother, crucial for individuation and separation from the mother.

The classical developmental schema for normal development will now be reviewed as a basis for comparison and contrast with other two theoretical views. The classical theorists have proposed that, at the outset of life, the ego and the id are not separated. This has been termed an undifferentiated phase. The infant is in a phase of primary narcissism, to use Freud's term, and in this period the infant feels himself to be the source of all satisfaction. Such a concept precludes an object relation. This conceptualization is important to keep in mind when distinguishing it from the Kleinian view, for the Kleinians propose that object relations exist from birth. Mahler conceptualized this first period as a normal autistic phase in which there is no distinction between inner and outer reality. According to Mahler, it extends to about eight weeks of life. The second phase, termed by Mahler the normal symbiotic phase, begins about the second month. In this period, the infant recognizes the identity of the mother as a need-satisfying object and reacts to her absence. The third stage, Mahler's milestone contribution, is the separation-individuation phase.

It was thought that the psychic structure was formed, for the most part, by six years of age. Hartmann, Kris, and Loewenstein (1946) maintain that the important elements of the personality structure are formed by five or six. However, the developmentalists on the current scene emphasize that psychological development does not end with childhood, but continues throughout the life span.

The three theoretical perspectives being considered hold different views as to the origins and causes of pathological deviation. In his early period, Freud distinguished transference neuroses from narcissistic neuroses. He described the narcissistic neuroses as ones in which object-relatedness is either nonexistent or hardly developed. To speak in current terms, it was conceptualized that a deficiency in the development of psychic structure took place initially within the matrix of the mother-infant relationship. It is upon this assumption that the self-psychological school evolved its particular conceptualization of pathology in structure formation. Within the classical school, it was the developmentalists who focused upon and considered the importance of a deficiency-based disturbance. The deficiency-based problems have been related to the preoedipal-dyadic stage of development; and it is to be considered distinct from the conflict-based neurosis, which has been related to oedipal-level pathology, also known as the infantile neurosis.

When Anna Freud conceptualized the mechanisms of defense, she focused on the conflict-derived sources of structure formation. Nevertheless, in her later writings, out of her observation of war-damaged children in the 1940s, she emphasized the importance of understanding pathological deviation in the preoedipal period, recognizing the important role of the earliest object relationships involved in primary structure formation. It was realized that when there is an inadequate resolution of the dyadic-stage issues, there will be interference with the resolution of oedipal problems. Moreover, it was recognized that the most severe pathology stems from the early failure in the preoedipal period.

Now I would like to raise the question as to how the theoretical formulations of normal and pathological development within the classical-developmental frame influence clinical or technical considerations. As attention became focused on the preoedipal period, there were attempts to relate the new knowledge about phase-derived developmental pathology to the therapeutic means by which it could be undone. Proponents of the developmental point of view looked at the possibility that the analyst might gratify or supply the patient with what was missing in his own development. They considered that a therapeutic psychoanalysis might revive and repeat the original developmental process now in a way that could be helpful. Needless to say, there was, and continues to be, an intense controversy about this issue in the traditional classical school. There are those who claim that such an approach tends to sidestep the importance of analyzing archaic conflicts, defenses, and ego states. Advocates of this position believe that psychoanalysis was not designed to deal with structural deficits. Freud (1919) clearly indicated that analytic neutrality meant not promoting or gratifying infantile aims and wishes. However, the following quote from Freud suggests that he, too, was aware that deviation from a strictly analytic approach was necessary with certain patients. I quote: "We cannot avoid taking some patients for treatment who are so helpless and incapable of ordinary life that for them one has to combine analytic with educative influence, and even with the majority, occasions now and then arise in which the physician is bound to take up the position of teacher and mentor."

In developing her concept of the therapeutic alliance, Elizabeth Zetzel (1969) maintained that the analyst must be like the good mother with intuitive, adaptive responses, that the therapeutic alliance was a recapturing of the very early relationship between mother and infant in which the infant turned to the mother for help in the way the patient now turned to the analyst. Ralph Greenson stated, and I quote: "Essentially, the humanness of the analyst is expressed in his compassion, concern, and therapeutic intent toward the patient" (p. 177). Not all within the classical group subscribe to these ideas. Charles Brenner believes that it would be better to deal with the patient's neediness and anxiety with interpretation, rather than with humanness and compassion. On this issue, therefore, it is clear that the classical perspective contains a spectrum of views.

Kleinian psychology will now be examined—its language, its schema, its timetable for normal development, and its understanding of pathological deviation. How its theoretical formulations are reflected in clinical practice will also be considered.

The language of Kleinian psychology is a concrete, vivid, colorful one. Melanie Klein developed her language of part-objects and bodily functions in her work with small children. It has been said by some that Klein created a language that is understandable to the infant inside the patient.

It is crucial to give the Kleinian definition of what an object is. The term object is used for the child's caretaker from the beginning of life through all of the succeeding stages of development: first of all, the object is seen as a part-object (e.g., as a breast), and then finally as someone who can be distinguished from the self and internalized in the process of identification.

Klein's first stage of development was termed the paranoid-schizoid position—paranoid because of the persecution fear and schizoid because of the splitting that occurs. Splitting is defined as that process by which the ideal object (the mother who gratifies) and the persecutor (the mother who frustrates) are to be kept apart, and various means like projection, introjections, and projective identification are used to attain this end. Projective identification, an important concept in Kleinian theory, can be defined as one of the early defense mechanisms of the paranoid-schizoid position in which the infant, in omnipotent fantasy, projects parts of himself, and sometimes the whole of himself, into his objects for his own safety or to control his objects.

Klein's second developmental stage has been termed the depressive position. The adjective depressive was selected for this stage because it aptly describes the predominant affect. The child now has to deal with the fear that his destructiveness has possibly damaged or destroyed the object of his love and dependence, an object now perceived as a whole person toward whom he has ambivalent feelings. A major group of defenses used to deny the feeling of ambivalence have been termed manic defenses.

After this brief introduction to Kleinian language, let us turn our attention to the Kleinian schema for normal development. It is important to note that while the classical analysts launch the infant in an undifferentiated state in which the id and the ego are not separated and where there is no distinction between inner and outer reality, the Kleinians insist that the ego—synonymous with the self—exists from birth, that the infant from the beginning is capable of forming object relations, can experience anxiety, have fantasies, and use defense mechanisms. Defense mechanisms, incidentally, are experienced as the fantasy of pushing something out and introjections as taking something in.

The basis for all conflict, according to Kleinian theory, is the struggle between the life and death instincts, and it is already operative during birth. Birth is experienced as trauma and attack which, in turn, leads to persecutory anxiety in relation to the external world. Freud, earlier, had proposed that aggression was a manifestation of a death instinct which eventuated in the destruction of life. However, today, while most classical analysts view aggression as a primary instinct, they do not believe in the death instinct; their interpretations usually incorporate the idea that aggression is activated by some external stimulus, and the purpose of these interpretations is to liberate and bring into focus the repressed rage of the patient. The Kleinians tend to focus more on the hostile, destructive nature of man than the classical analysts do, and they tend to stress aggression as a primary drive rather than a reaction to some assault from external reality. The psyche in early infancy is thought to be dominated by aggressive fantasies motivated by greed, envy, oral and anal sadism: the frustrating breast becomes a bad breast and is experienced as persecuting. It becomes the prototype for later persecutory objects.

As I indicated earlier, the Kleinians have termed the first stage of life the paranoid-schizoid position. Normally, this characterizes the infant's first three months. It is dominated by fears of annihilation and fragmentation.

In the depressive period which follows, the infant now recognizes his mother, as well as others, as whole persons. The child now has to deal with his ambivalence. He feels guilty because he hates the mother he loves. This makes him depressed and increases his need to make reparation. The reparative efforts are an attempt to restore the lost or damaged object, as well as an attempt to overcome the child's own destructive instincts. It is interesting to note that, according to Kleinian theory, the shift to heterosexuality and full oedipal love derives from the wish to make reparation.

Unlike the theoretical views of the other two groups where the oedipal complex occurs in the three-and-a-half- to five-year-old range, Klein wrote that a full development of oedipal conflicts is seen in the first year of life with the beginning of the depressive position. The infant is said to be innately aware at this time of the genitalia of both sexes and of parental sexual intercourse. This awareness leads him to feel deprived, jealous, and envious. In retaliation, the infant in fantasy attacks and destroys the parents.

What makes for pathological deviation within the Kleinian theoretical framework? Melanie Klein gave envy a central place in her schema for understanding pathological deviation. When envy outbalances the wish to preserve the love of the object, there is interference with the forward-moving developmental processes. The introjections of the good object is essential for positive developmental growth, and this internalization of the good object can only occur when the individual feels he has goodness within himself. He must first discover his good self before he can find his good object. The feelings of envy interfere with this feeling of goodness, and it interferes with the development of self-esteem. Also, there must be a predominance of good experience over bad with the objects in his world if the child is to progress from the paranoid-schizoid position to the depressive one.

In Kleinian theory it is important to note that major milestones in mental development are to be achieved within the first year of life. Even the oedipal conflict is believed to be present in rudimentary form in this earliest period. This is probably one of the reasons why Melanie Klein thought it should be possible to analyze children of three years or even younger.

As to the nature of analytic interpretations that are given, Kleinians tend to interpret directly that which Freudian would call id content. The classical analysts, on the other hand approach the unconscious through the analysis of resistance.

The Kleinians have also stressed that in dealing with the defenses of the patient, it is the fantasy of the defense that must be interpreted. For example, the defense mechanism projection might be expressed as a fantasy in which the painful thought or idea is expelled by an evacuating process, often an anal one. In addition, the Kleinians have also indicated that the interpretation of defenses is not effective unless they are interpreted in the context of what the patient feels and does to the analyst in the transference by means of projective identification. This led to broadening the concept of countertransference in order to use the analyst's feelings as a source of information about the patient. Apparently, Melanie Klein (1988) felt that this broader concept of countertransference and projective identification could be misused. A story that has been told about this concerns a young analyst who was being supervised by Melanie Klein. When he told her that he was confused by the patient, and, therefore, interpreted to her that she had projected her confusion into him, Melanie Klein replied, "No, dear, you *are* confused" (p. 10).

We will turn now to the theory of self-psychology. Like the innovators of the other two theoretical groups, self-psychology theorists have also developed their own language. As mentioned earlier, the term object was introduced very early in psychoanalytic theory to stand for the sexual object, and later for the loved person. Kohut (1978) introduced the term *self-object*, which he defined as an object experienced as part of the self. The control over a self-object is, and I quote Kohut, "closer to the concept of the control which a grown-up expects to have over his mind and body than it is to the concept of the control he expects to have over others" (p. 413). Kohut described two kinds of self-objects. One he termed "mirroring self-objects"—those who respond and confirm a child's innate sense of vigor and greatness. The second he called "idealized parent images"—those whom the child can respect and with whom he can merge as an image of calmness and omnipotence.

Another important Kohutian terms is "transmuting internalization." It is through the process of transmuting internalization that new psychological structure is built. The process occurs through innumerable micro-internalizations in which the patient takes in the anxiety-reducing aspects of the psychoanalyst's image and makes them part of his own psychological equipment. This idea, incidentally, is not dissimilar to the classical concept of mutative interpretation, introduced by Strachey, in which the patient internalizes the mature, less punitive superego of the analyst.

Kohut noted two types of transference that emerge in psychoanalytic treatment. One was termed the "idealizing transference." This is a state in which the psyche assigns a part of the lost experience of narcissistic perfection to an archaic, rudimentary self-object—the idealized parent imago. Since all bliss and power now reside in the idealized object, the child feels empty and powerless when he is separated from it and he attempts, therefore, to maintain a continuous union with it. The second transference reaction was labeled "mirror transference." Kohut used this term to describe the revival in the treatment situation of the childhood need for a source of accepting, confirming reflection.

In 1971 when Kohut wrote *The Psychology of the Self* he still believed in the tripartite model, including the term ego, but by 1977 with the publication of his *Restoration of the Self*, the tripartite model as well as the term ego faded from his writings. His concept of the self, however, had grown in importance from viewing it originally as a mental content along with ego, id, and superego in the psychic apparatus to its new position as a supraordinate agency in the mind. Kohut spoke of a new term, "the nuclear self." Kohut conceptualized the self as a "bipolar structure." At one point, he hypothesized archaic ambitions, at the other, archaic ideals; with a "tension arc" between them which would enhance the development of the child's skills and talents—rudimentary skills and talents that will gradually blossom into those employed by the mature adult.

The last definitional note I would like to make relates to Kohut's conceptualization of "destructive rage," or narcissistic rage. According to Kohut, destructive rage is always motivated by an injury to the self, for Kohut believed that man's destructiveness is secondary, that it comes about as a result of the failure of the child's self-objects to meet his needs for empathy and acceptance. What is likely to be considered a ranting, raving, instinctually aggressive infant in the other theoretical groups is viewed by Kohut as an assertive baby whose behavior reflects the firmness with which he makes his demands upon his self-objects. According to Kohut, true destructive rage is the result of a need for omnipotent control over a self-object that has chronically and traumatically failed him in childhood.

Kohut has proposed a schema for the normal development of the self. He maintained that while there are indications that ambitions and ideals are acquired in early infancy, the major part of the infant's grandiosity consolidates into nuclear ambitions in the second, third, and fourth years of life. The major portion of the idealized goal structures are acquired later in childhood, probably in the fourth, fifth, and sixth years of life. He claims that the earlier parts of the self are derived from the relationship with the maternal self-object, and later acquired parts may relate to parental figures of either sex. The caretaking individual who serves as the mirroring, empathic, approving self-object helps the child establish his grandiose, exhibitionistic self, to use Kohut's language. But the caretaking individual who responds empathically to the child by enjoying the child's idealization of him and a wish to merge with him leads to the establishment of the child's idealized parent imago.

Kohut suggests that the developmental progression is from the maternal self-object, who mirrors the child, to the paternal self-object, who is idealized by the child. According to Kohut, if the child experiences failure with the first self-object, the mother, this can be remedied by a success with the second one, usually the father. As for the oedipal stage, self-psychologists claim that it is more pleasurable than heretofore believed. When problems exist, it is the result of parental failure in empathy.

In classical theory when problems exist, it is due mainly to conflict in the child. Self-psychologists stress the fact that normal childhood development depends on the fulfillment of various and continuing developmental needs that go far beyond the libidinal and aggressive drive wishes. In fact, the need for self-objects, according to Kohut, persists throughout one's life span.

In order to understand the self-psychologist's view of pathological deviation, I would like to underscore the fact that this theory grew out of a study of the narcissistic personality disorder. This disturbance is viewed as a narcissistic injury which affects the individual's self-esteem or self-regard. In his attempt to bolster his self-esteem, he might search out others who still mirror him because he is unable to regulate his own self-esteem; or he might attempt to merge with an idealized self-object.

Kohut has given a central role to the concept of empathy in the psychoanalytic process. He has specified that the narcissistically disordered individual has not had adequate empathic mothering in his early developmental years, so Kohut devised certain variations of technique in order to provide that kind of experience for his patients. Paul Ornstein, another self-psychologist, stated: "Kohut often provides the patient with narcissistic sustenance through approval, mirroring, and echoing." Kohut has proposed postponing interpretation until the analyst has established himself with the patient as an empathic self-object. He is critical of those analysts who skip over an important stage in treatment: a stage of understanding, defined by Kohut, and I quote—"the stage of the endless empathic echo or merger with the patient." He goes on to state: "The analyst will have to realize that a patient whose childhood self-object has failed dramatically in this area will require long periods of 'only' understanding before the second step [a dynamic, genetic] interpretation . . . can be usefully and acceptably undertaken" (p. 413).

Kohut has denied that he deviates from established analytic technique, but his disclaimer notwithstanding, Kohutians, with their special handling of the mirroring and idealizing transference, their emphasis on allowing the self-object transference to develop, and their special definition of empathy and its role in the curative process, pose a variation in theory and in technique, at the very least in the timing of interpretations.

This concludes an abbreviated review of three theoretical perspectives. In summary, now, I will compare and contrast the theories, following the general topical outline: namely, the theoretical schema for normal development and pathological deviation and the ways in which theory influences technique.

In regard to the schema for normal development, there is controversy as to what the state of the human psyche is at birth—the Kleinians postulating a functioning, separated self and the classical developmentalists conceptualizing an undifferentiated state. The self-psychologists dismiss the issue by disclaiming an interest in the rudimentary ego of the infant. The psychology of the self, according to Kohut, begins with the establishment of the self; prior to that, Kohut bows to drive psychology to provide explanatory concepts.

Regarding the developmental timetable, the Kleinians have accelerated and condensed progression through the psychosexual stages so that even the oedipal period is thought to have its roots in the first year of life. The classical and Kohutian groups are more or less in agreement with regard to the sequential pattern of the developmental timetable. Where they differ is in the relative importance they place on the different phases. The classical theorists, prior to the contributions of the developmentalists, especially that of M. Mahler, tended to focus more on the resolution of the oedipal period as the crucial milestone in development. Kohut, on the other hand, emphasized that the preoedipal years called for indispensable empathic parenting if a sound, cohesive self were to develop. The oedipal period, according to this view, was only problematic if the earlier phase lacked empathic understanding from important self-objects.

The development of aggression is also viewed differently by each theoretical perspective, depending in part on their different understanding of the basic nature of man. The classical analytic position holds that the aggressiveness in man has instinctual roots which have to be tamed and, at times, repressed or sublimated in the socialization process. The Kleinian school also subscribes to the notion that aggression is an instinct, but it tends to focus more on the hostile, destructive nature of man than the other two groups, and stress aggression as a primary drive rather than as a reaction to environmental pressure. Kohut, for his part, discounts the idea that aggression is instinctual; rather, he views it as a reaction to unempathic parenting.

Another comparison that pertains to normal development is how it relates to the development of self-esteem. In classical psychoanalysis, it is hypothesized that the child begins life in an undifferentiated phase in which he attributes, via his omnipotence, all satisfaction to himself, then moves to a stage in which he perceives his parents as omnipotent and he tries, through introjections, to share their omnipotence again. This formulation can be likened to the Kohutian concept of the purpose served by the idealized self-object. In both these theoretical groups, the individual must find his good object before he can establish his good self. The reverse is true in Kleinian psychology; the Kleinians believe that the person must first discover his good self before he can find his good object. I would also like to note here that the classical analysts concern themselves with whole objects, the Kleinians with part objects and whole objects, and the Kohutians with self-objects.

One final comparison: There is a parallel between the Kleinian concept of projective identification and the Kohutian concept of self-object. In each, there is an internalization of an important object over which one needs to exert control. The forerunner for this process is contained in the classical Freudian concept of object cathexis.

Now let us examine the ways in which these groups view pathology. Pathology, according to the classical school, is understood primarily in terms of conflict. In the structural neuroses, the conflict resides within the three agencies of the mind or within the ego itself. The classical analyst focuses on the conflicts around the preoedipal phase and the oedipal complex. Kohut centered his attention fully on preoedipal issues and stated that oedipal problems mainly stemmed from unresolved preoedipal difficulties. For the self-psychologists, the nuclear pathology in narcissistic disturbances is an absence or deficit in the individual's psychological structure that maintains self-esteem and self-cohesion.

Freudians believe that traumatic events in early childhood have a crucial influence in the development of an individual's personality. The Kohutians think that if the individual has a cohesive self due to good parenting, then serious traumata in the child can be adequately coped with without significant disturbance. The Kleinian school pays less attention to environmental stress and trauma than either of the other two.

In the Kleinian theory, pathology is related to an increase in the strength of the death of instinct or an increase in hatred and envy in the infant leading to a greater persecutory anxiety. The primitive oedipal situation expressed in oral, anal, and phallic terms leads to the intense conflicts within the child in the first year. The Kleinians tend to attribute pathological deviation to a predominance of poor mothering experiences over good mothering experiences. So they do not dismiss environmental influences.

We now come to the last issue, raised at the outset of this paper, namely, is it possible to unify the three theories in one? Or, do we have to adhere strictly to one specific theoretical stance in conceptualizing what goes on with our patients? No easy answer comes to mind. Certainly, each body of theory has made its special contribution to understanding psychological development. Classical psychoanalytic theory has probably provided the broadest, most inclusive framework; whereas Kohut has deepened our understanding of the narcissistic personality, its development, and its treatment, especially in highlighting the importance in relating to the patient exclusively through his subjectivity. He has significantly helped us focus more on concepts like empathy and introspection. The Kleinians have certainly increased our knowledge and understanding of the primitive dark side of man's nature—his greed, envy, and destructive impulses—and magnified our awareness of primitive mechanisms of defense.

So can we pick and choose from each theory as the clinical material demands? We do to some extent, because each one has broadened our knowledge; however, there are certain inherent pitfalls in such random selection. Certain mutually exclusive concepts cannot coexist within a single unitary theory, because they are inconsistent and contradictory. One example relates to technique.

Each theoretical position demands that we use a special technique in the treatment of the patient. The classical technique encourages the development of a transference neurosis in which there is a delay in interpretation until transferences are clear and well formed. Interpreting the negative transferences as they arise is also important in the classical technique. Kleinians, on the other hand, believe that there is a full transference development on the first day of treatment, and deep interpretations can be given at the beginning of treatment. The self-psychologists take a different point of view. They feel that a long time is required for a transference to develop before interpretations are offered; moreover, they encourage the development of an idealizing and mirroring self-object transference. They do not analyze conflict, and they do not interpret negative transference, which has high priority in the classical and Kleinian schools.

Clearly it is helpful to know the different theoretical languages of psychoanalysts. However, there are some hazards involved in an eclectic approach, which can result in disjointed theoretical speculations and treatment approach. These hazards remind me of a story which demonstrates how mismanaged and disjointed communication can get when one thinks that he understands a language and, in fact, does not.

The story takes place in a very old Victorian hotel, very upper class, very British. A young man has just entered the lobby—an imposing, regal-looking lobby with potted palms and straight-back chairs lining the long hall to the reception desk. And there are a number of old ladies sitting in these chairs. One of them catches the young man's eye and he walks toward her. At first, she does not seem to notice him. Nevertheless, he addresses her: "Pardon me, Madam, your face is very familiar." Whereupon, the old lady looks at him and says: "Eh-h-h?!!" The young man leans closer to her, speaking louder this time. "Madam, your face—your face is very familiar." The woman pulls out a large hearing horn from her embroidered satchel and places it in her ear. "Speak up, young man. I can't hear you." The young man leans even closer, and says: "Madam, your face—your face is very familiar." "Louder, louder!" she cries. The young man is shouting now. "Madam, madam, your face is very familiar." "Oh-h-h-h!" she exclaims with the glowing satisfied look of recognition. "I found it in the woods, all covered with moss. And I dug it up and took it home and buried it in the garden; there it grew and it grew and it grew until it covered the whole house."

Chapter Two

Four Psychoanalytic Perspectives

This research study was designed to test two main hypotheses: 1) there are detectable differences in interpretive style among classical Kleinian, Kohutian, and Kernbergian analysts; and 2) the nature of these differences can be discerned and described. The methodology consists of three phases of data collection. The statistical findings are presented along with clinical examples, followed by a discussion of their implications.

Psychoanalysis provides a wide umbrella for a varied spectrum of theoretical orientations. It has been suggested that the commonalities among different analytic groups are greater than their stated differences, that in the consulting room, distinctions fade and one cannot discern one analytic perspective from another (Wallerstein, 1988). In this paper, we shall describe a research project we designed to study such a hypothesis, that is, we attempted to determine whether therapeutic interventions by psychoanalysis reelect their theoretical perspective and, if they do, what implications may be drawn about the nature of these differences. As the object of our study, we chose four psychoanalytic perspectives: classical, Kleinian, Kohutian, and Kernbergian.

In our review of the literature, we found no references to any rigorous, systematic research that investigated the specific ways in which analysts apply their theoretical perspective to treatment. In 1938, Glover formulated a rather lengthy, detailed questionnaire in which he attempted to learn how members of the British Psychoanalytic Society actually conducted a psychoanalysis (Glover, 1955). The questionnaire covered such issues as the neutrality of the analyst, the focus on transference interpretations, the manner of interpreting anxiety, the use of reassurance, the terminology used, the emphasis on childhood memories and reconstruction, and the degree of friendliness and spontaneity on the part of the analyst. Glover found there was general agreement that the analysis of transference was the main therapeutic aim. However, he found wide variation on matters pertaining to the technique of interpretation, its mode, length, timing, and depth. He found that the reassurance problem was clearly unresolved. The technique of interpretation, he concluded, was more an individual matter. There was marked disagreement on the question of etiology, the nature of anxiety, and the significance of aggressive impulses. Glover attributed such disagreement to individual differences. He did not attempt to make distinctions on the basis of one's theoretical perspective, as we are attempting to do, even though it is well known that in the 1940s there were splits in the British Psychoanalytic Society between those who were followers of Melanie Klein and those who gathered about Anna Freud.

There is an oft-cited 1950 study by Fiedler who purported to examine whether therapeutic relationships were a function of theoretical school or the therapist's experience and expertise. His results indicated that there were more similarities among therapists of greater experience than among those of a given theoretical orientation. He studied the psychoanalytic, Adlerian, and nondirective therapeutic approaches. Fiedler drew the conclusion that the relationship was all important, that it was the primary cause of psychological change. However, his conclusion was not warranted by the study he conducted. He had no criteria for successful treatment outcome, nor did he make any attempt to measure it.

In 1978, Lakin and Lebovitz carried out a study which attempted to explore the effect of the therapist's "conceptualizing set" on the way he viewed the patient. They used three groups of therapists, representing the psychoanalytic, the nondirective, and the eclectic points of view. It was a limited project in the sense that the subjects were given global material about a patient and asked to free associate as to how they would "think about this person." The researchers found that psychoanalysts were most productive in their associations and showed more concern about genetic determinants and less concern about being in error of making contradictory statements than did the other groups. The other two groups showed certain characteristic differences. While this study sheds no light on the subject matter we have selected to examine, it does suggest that certain inclinations or biases are present and a function of one's theoretical training.

The only relevant literature that specifically relates to the issues we have raised in our study consists of theoretical and clinical papers and books written by proponents of each of the theoretical groups under study, as well as those that attempt a comparative analysis of two or more of the groups (Freud, 1914, 1919; A. Freud, 1936; Fenichel, 1945; Klein, 1955; H. Segal, 1964, 1977; Blum, 1981; Kernberg, 1969, 1974, 1975, 1979, 1982, 1984; Kohut, 1971, 1977, 1978a, 1978b, 1979, 1984; Greenberg, 1974; Pulver, 1987; Wallerstein 1985, 1986; Reed, 1987). None of these contributions made any pretense of studying the differences with any kind of formal systematic methodology.

Our research project was begun in 1980. At that time, one of us was invited to present to a seminar on dream analysis, sponsored by the Los Angeles Psychoanalytic Society, an analytic session that would demonstrate how analysis of a dream advanced the analytic process. Before the actual interpretations were stated, the members of their seminar group were asked how they understood the dream and how they might interpret it to the patient. It became apparent that there were sharp differences in the way they would approach this patient, and that the differences seemed to relate to the theoretical schools to which these analysts belonged. Some of them were Kleinians, others were Kohutian. The majority held more traditional Freudian views.

When we later discussed the variation in interpretive responses to the dream, we were intrigued with the idea of using this method to study the differences among the various theoretical groups. We came up with the idea of using this analytic session with the dream content as a form of projective test for analysts of distinctively different analytic views. That skeleton of an idea was fleshed out over the next eight years to take the form we have described in this paper.

Methodology

The method we devised to study the differences in therapeutic intervention consisted of three phases.

1. Fourteen experienced psychoanalysts reviewed a detailed account of an analytic hour, plus a brief summary of the patient's history and a year and one-half of analytic treatment. The interpretive comments that were made in the analytic session were withheld from the material these analysts received. Each analyst was directed to formulate the kind of interpretation he would make and where in the hour he would have made it. Each line of the summarized hour was numbered to make it easy for the analyst to note where he would intervene. There were three analysts who represented the self-psychological point of view, four drawn from the Kleinian group, four from the classical point of view, and three who were identified as Kernbergians.
2. Twenty-four raters with fifteen or more years of experience, also drawn from one of the four theoretical groups without any prior knowledge of who made these interpretations.
3. Ten analysts were selected from the twenty-four raters because of their unusual accuracy in their identifications or their special knowledge about the differences among the groups. A statistical analysis revealed that there were one or two analysts in each theoretical group

whose theoretical orientation most of our raters were able to identify correctly. We termed such analysts our prototypic analysts. We asked our select ten-member group to explain why these prototypic analysts' interpretations were characteristic of their particular theoretical group. These ten analysts were provided with rating scales to help guide them in their explanatory efforts. They were required to rate the influence that certain factors might have on classifying the interpretations of a particular analyst in terms of a particular theoretical group: 1) the manner in which defense and resistance is interpreted; 2) the way in which transference is interpreted; 3) the focus on the patient's vulnerability; 4) the focus on the patient's primitive impulses; 5) the focus on the patient's hostile aggressiveness; and 6) the use of special catchwords or phraseology. Each analyst was asked to rate these items on a 9-3 scale and to explain why he rated them this way. In addition, we instructed these analysts not to feel restricted by the rating scales and to express any and all thoughts they might have about the material

Limitations

First and foremost, this is a simulated experience for the analyst participants. We have no way of determining whether their interpretations are indeed the ones they would have made in an *in vivo* session. It has been suggested that the analyst participant might have viewed his task as a test situation; and he might have made a greater effort to present interpretations that most clearly and effectively reflected his theoretical point of view. Moreover, the written account of the session is necessarily static—the interpretations cannot alter the course of the hour, for they cannot possibly influence the patient's associations or effect behavioral and/or emotional changes. As we have attempted to make very clear, this study does not purport to compare the efficacy of the different treatment approaches; rather, it is an attempt to examine how analysts with differing theoretical perspectives will interpret the same clinical material.

Another artifact concerns the case itself. Our case has a narcissistic personality disorder. Perhaps a different type of case would have elicited very different kinds of interpretations. Despite our awareness of these inherent weaknesses, we considered our methodology sufficiently sensitive to answer some of the research questions that we posed.

Clinical Data

The following account is a summary of the clinical material used in the research project.

It consists of a brief history of the patient and a detailed account of an analytic session with all comments and interpretations of the analyst withheld.

The patient was a research scientist, twenty-eight years of age. He was phobic about many things: strange places, small social groups, and the people with whom he worked. When he came to see me, a prominent symptom was his extreme separation anxiety from his parents. Although he lived alone, he became frightened when they went out of town, or if he did.

Although of high intelligence, he had severe learning difficulties. In school, he was unable to make friends or play. He shielded himself in an arrogant, superior mental cloak, and tended to view others with condescension and contempt.

His mother was clinically depressed during his infancy. She spent most of her time with her husband, giving the infant little attention. During his growing up years, he had few friendships, and those relationships were disturbed ones. The two close relationships he had with girls were sadomasochistic. He treated women in an arrogant, contemptuous manner, belittling them constantly, and finally leaving them. In his adult years, he depreciated his mother, whom he identified with black people.

In the analysis, he showed an attitude of arrogance, superiority, and depreciation. He could insult me without shame or guilt. The slightest experience of hurt threatened his fragile state and made him feel as if he were disintegrating.

The following is a summarized account of one session that occurred a year and a half after the beginning of his analysis. The day before this session, the patient had come to his hour to find that I had another patient in the office and it was necessary for me to send him away. Two weeks before he had told me he had to cancel his Monday hour. He had meant to say three weeks instead of two. When I informed him of his error, he was both cordial and polite.

When he came for his session the following day, he said that although he had shown no distress the day before, he had in actuality hidden his feelings. He had had a great deal to tell me and felt "pissed off, " but he could not support his argument about Monday, because he thought he had given me mixed messages. He admitted he might have made a mistake.

He had met with his boss about research. It was not good. If grants were not forthcoming, he might not be able to remain in the department. He wanted to know how I would feel if he had to go somewhere else. "Are you concerned?" he asked me. He started an argument with me to put the analysis down; then he indicated it was also a matter of concern to him, but, in his words, "I guess I don't want to give you that. Like I said yesterday when I left your office, 'Don't worry, it's okay.' When I confess this to you, it is like walking on thin ice." If I knew that he felt rejected and hurt yesterday, it would be like arming me. It was important to him that I not know and that he not know that he felt let down. His immediate response was, "I don't give a shit. Okay, that's great, I'm busy anyway." He explained that it was too dangerous to reveal that he was weak and needy, that he needs people badly. "The needy person gets fucked. Neediness sucks! I detest babies and their whimpering neediness!"

He then proceeded to give me a detailed account of a dream about the murder of his tailor, who was black. I started to speak to him about the dream, but at this point the patient, thinking that I was going to give an interpretation of the dream, said he turned himself off. He said to himself: "This is going to be wrong, insignificant. I won't listen. I should begin by exercising at home. I should start chinning. I stopped listening entirely." It was now the end of the session.

Results of Phases I and II

1. The answer to the first research question we posed is yes. The question, you will recall, was: "Are there detectable differences among the self-psychological, Kleinian, classical, and Kernbergian analysts in the way they interpret clinical material in the analytic hour?" We found that all four groups of our analyst participants were correctly identified at the .05 level of statistical significance. Therefore, we were able to reject the null hypothesis as it pertains to these groups. They are sufficiently different in the way they give interpretations to be identifiable beyond the point of chance selection.
2. Certain analysts in our study were consistently identified as belonging to a particular theoretical group. As was noted earlier, we termed these analysts five in number, our prototypic analysts. With the exception of the Kernbergians, the prototypic analysts in the other groups were clearly identifiable at the /.001 level of confidence. The Kernbergians just missed being selected at the .05 level.
3. Our theoretical groups were hierarchically ordered in the degree to which they were identifiable. The Kleinian interpretations were the most easily identifiable. Next in line were the Self-psychological group. Accuracy was lower for the Classical and Kernbergian groups, and the difference between them was not significant. The overall difference among the groups was significant at the .0001 level of confidence, a very respectable statistical standard.
4. When our raters (twenty-four in number) made errors, those errors were not random. In the Kohutian group, 49 percent were categorized incorrectly. Of that 49 percent, 71.4 percent were rated as Classical. This is significant at the .001 percent level of confidence. In the Kleinian group, only 30 percent were incorrectly identified; and on the 30

percent, 62 percent were judged to be Kernbergian. This is significant at the .003 level. In the classical group, 56 percent were rated incorrectly, and of this group, 51 percent were rated as Kohutians and 37 percent were rated as Kernbergian. In the Kernbergian group, 65 percent of our raters were incorrect in judging the Kernbergian interpretations. However, 74 percent of those judged incorrectly were judged as Classical. This result is significant at the .001 level.

5. The responses of the fourteen analysts were highly different in the way in which they were rated. The statistical significance was at the .05 level. In other words, not only were the analysts of three of the groups correctly identifiable in terms of their theoretical group, but all fourteen analysts, irrespective of their group, were significantly different from one another.
6. Kleinians made twice as many interpretations as the members of the three other groups. They also gave longer and more detailed interpretations of the dream material.
7. There were differences among the groups related to the degree of certainty and conviction with which the interpretations were offered. The prototypic Kleinian and Kohutian analysts stated all their interpretations in a definitive manner with a sense of certainty and conviction, whereas 29 percent of the prototypic classical interpretations and 33 and 2/3 percent of the prototypic Kernbergian interpretations were offered in the form of a question or a statement containing an element of doubt.
8. The interpretations of the majority of our fourteen analysts tended to be offered at the same specific points in the summarized analytic hour. Our theoretical groups were hierarchically ordered in the degree to which they were identifiable. The Kleinian interpretations were the most easily identifiable. Next in line were the self-psychological. Accuracy was lower for the Classical and Kernbergian groups, and the difference between them was not significant. The overall difference among the groups was significant at the /.0001 level of confidence, a very respectable statistical standard.
9. When our raters (twenty-four in number) made errors, those errors were not random. In the Kohutian group, 49 percent were categorized incorrectly. Of that 49 percent, 71.4 percent were rated as Classical. This is significant at the .001 level of confidence. In the Kleinian group, only 30 percent were incorrectly identified and of this 30 percent, 62 percent were judged to be Kernbergian. This is significant at the .005 level. In the Classical group, 56 percent were rated incorrectly, and of this group, 51 percent were rated as Kohutian and 37 percent were rated as Kernbergian. In the Kernbergian group, 65 percent of our raters were incorrect in judging the Kernbergian interpretations.

However, 74 percent of those judged incorrectly were judged as Classical. This result is significant at the .001 level. The responses of the fourteen analysts were highly different in the way in which they were rated. The statistical significance was at the .05 level. In other words, not only were the analysts of three of the groups correctly identifiable in terms of their theoretical, but all fourteen analysts, irrespective of their group, were significantly different from one another.

10. Kleinians made twice as many interpretations as the members of the three other groups.
11. They also gave longer and more detailed interpretations of the dream material. There were differences among the groups related to the degree of certainty and conviction with which the interpretations were offered. The other prototypic Kleinian and Kohutian analysts stated all their interpretations in a definitive manner with a sense of certainty and conviction, whereas 29 percent of the prototypic classical interpretations and 33 and 2/3 percent of the prototypic Kernbergian interpretations were offered in the form of a question or a statement obtaining an element of doubt.
12. The interpretations of the majority of our fourteen analysts tended to be offered at the same specific points in the summarized analytic hour. Clearly, the obtained statistical results indicated discernible differences among our theoretical groups, but they did not indicate the nature of these differences. This led into another phase of our research in order to determine what made for the differences. Before discussing this major portion of our work, let us examine the above findings.

Closely related to the primary result that there are significant differences in the interpretive approach is the finding that a certain analyst or analysts in each group were clearly more identifiable than others. We have called these analysts prototypic, and we have inferred that their interpretations are sufficiently representative of their particular theoretical group to subject them to closer scrutiny. That our prototypic Kleinian analyst was selected correctly by all twenty-four raters and that our Kohutian was correctly identified by 91 percent of our raters strongly suggests a clear-cut gestalt in the way they formulate their interpretations. We shall discuss the elements that make up that gestalt in a later section.

We found that our theoretical groups were hierarchically ordered in the degree to which they were identifiable: first, Kleinian; second, Kohutian; last, Classical and Kernbergian. As with our prototypic analyst, we can assume that Kleinians and Kohutians provide a more recognizable and perhaps more simplified theoretical schema. The greater difficulty in identifying Classical and Kernbergian interpretations evokes several possible explanations: 1) the Classical analysts may incorporate a greater blend of other theoretical schools and adhere less rigidly to a particular focus; 2) in the words of some Classical adherents, Classical theory may encompass greater explanatory power over a broader range of psychic phenomena (Hartmann, 1939, Rapaport, 1951); 3) the Classical analysts' interpretations are characteristically and purposefully more tenuous and, therefore, more difficult to categorize; 4) Kernberg's ideas are less well known.

Another finding was that when our raters made errors, those errors were not random. For example, our raters tended to mistake Kleinian interpretations for Classical ones. Perhaps this should not surprise us. It is also well known that he has used the Kleinian construct of projective identification in his conceptualizations (Kernberg, 1987), and that he stresses the importance of analyzing the patient's underlying oral, destructive rage (Kernberg, 1975). However, Kernberg himself maintains he is not Kleinian in his orientation; rather, that he attempts to synthesize Edith Jacobson's ideas on object relations with ego psychology, and that he conducts a traditional Classical analysis with patients who are not borderline or severely narcissistically disordered (Kernberg, 1979). Our findings suggest Kernberg is correct in categorizing himself as a classical analyst, and there is a widespread misconception about his work.

Over half of the classical analysts were mistakenly rated as Kernbergian or self-psychological, and only rarely as Kleinian, suggesting that Classical analysts have incorporated ideas from these other schools into their work. Inasmuch as raters tended to identify Kernbergian interventions as Classical, the likelihood is that the self-psychological school has had the greater impact in affecting the Classical analysts' work. We also found significant variability among all the analysts despite the fact that they could be identified as belonging to a particular theoretical group. This suggests that each analyst has his own unique blend or various theoretical ideas, although he may predominantly use a given model in his work with patients.

Our finding that the Kleinians gave twice as many interpretations as analysts from the other three groups was striking, and we questioned Kleinian and ex-Kleinian analysis about this clear-cut result. We were told that, indeed, Kleinians in training are taught in their supervision to intervene actively and frequently. While our study did not address the question of what difference the differences made, we inquired informally as to what effect Kleinian analysts thought the frequency of intervention might have on the patient. We were told that if the analyst is sensitive, the patient is excited and pleased by the active participation of the analyst; but the patient might experience the interventions as dogmiatic and doctrinaire if these interpretations are given by an insensitive therapist.

Another result pertained to the degree of certainty and conviction with which the interpretations were offered. Our findings clearly indicated that the prototypic Kleinian and Kohutian interpretations were offered with conviction and certainty, whereas in 30 percent of the classical and Kernbergian interpretations, the interventions were stated with an element of doubt or in the form of a question. Several of our raters independently, without the aid of statistical computations, noted the difference also. Depending on their theoretical point of view, this was sometimes mentioned in a pejorative way or as a laudable approach in treatment. The latter is reflected in the following comment; "Questions are a significant and judicial tool in classical psychoanalysis" (R. Zaitlin, rater). Furthermore, it was stated that the classical analyst attempts in this way to elicit material from the patient, rather than impose ideas on him. G. Aronson (rater, personal communication) has introduced the concept of privileged access to refer to the question of who is the one who knows what is in the patient's mind. In this context, it may be conjectured that assertive statements about what the patient is feeling or thinking designate the analyst as the one with privileged access, whereas an intervention that comes in the form of questioning views privileged access as residing in the patient. Two of our rater discussants have suggested that the more a psychoanalyst claims privileged access, the less he permits the patient to experience. An example can be drawn from the research material. In the analytic hour, the patient at one point asks the analyst, "Are you concerned?" Our prototypic classical analyst asked, "How do you think I feel?" Our prototypic Kohutian analyst stated, "I have a sense that you have an intensified need to be assured of my continued interest in you, that you mean something to me, and that you don't just disappear from my mind when you leave." Our prototypic Kernbergian did not intervene at this juncture, but another one of the Kernbergians did. The latter stated: "Perhaps you prefer to attribute this concern to me rather than yourself." We scored words such as "perhaps" or possibly as indicating an element of doubt in the proffered interpretation. Some of our Kleinian and self-psychologically oriented raters tended to be critical of the classical analyst's intervention, viewing it as vague, nebulous, and nondirective.

Let us consider the content of these four interpretations of the patient's question, "Are you concerned?" The Kohutian deals with it at face value and addresses himself to the patient's need to hold the analyst's interest—perhaps tuning into the experience near (Kohut, 1984). The classical analyst attempts to elicit the patient's thoughts and fantasies, perhaps to prepare for a transference interpretation. Both the Kleinian and the Kernbergian view the question as a projection. All are in keeping with the dictates of their theoretical model (Segal, 1964; Greenson, 1967; Kernberg, 1975).

Our last finding relates to the point of intervention. There tended to be clusters of interpretations at a given point in the analytic hour. Most of the analysts intervened after the patient asked, "Are you concerned?" They also intervened when the patient expressed his annoyance with the "whimpering neediness of infants." The analysts tended to comment on the patient's resistance to listening further at the end of the hour. All of the interventions tended to be transference interpretations, although each seemingly was molded by a specific theoretical focus. This finding coincides with the one reported by Glover (1955), who noted that the analysts in his study, regardless of their differing view on other variables, agreed that analysis of the transference was the most important aspect of the analytic process. As mentioned earlier, the Kleinians tended to interpret the dream material more than the other groups. One rationale that was presented by members of the other groups for not interpreting the dream is that they tended to withhold dream interpretations until presented with more associations to the dream, which they felt were lacking in the protocol.

Results of Phase III and Their Implications

Each prototypic analyst provided a recognizable gestalt in his interpretive style and content. Our select group of raters concluded that the Kohutian and the Kleinian were most easily identifiable. Many times, they could only identify the classical analysts by exclusion; but with careful attention to detail, the characteristic elements of the other two, like the classical and Kernbergian were also identifiable. Before describing these gestalts and their component parts, we shall present the results obtained from scoring our rating scales. We shall cite findings only where there was 60 percent or better agreement among the ten raters with regard to the interpretations of a prototypic analyst on a given variable.

The first variable, the manner in which defense and resistance is interpreted, attained our consensual standard in the case of the prototypic classical analysts. Eighty percent of our raters gave classical analytic interpretations a score of 4 with regard to the focus on defense and resistance. In the case of Kernberg, there was a split consensus; 60 percent gave Kernbergian interpretations a rating of 2, and 40 percent gave them a rating of 3. First, we reviewed the classical analysts' emphasis on defense and resistance. We noted a repeated attempt to look at the clinical data in terms of the patient's conflict and his resistance to looking at this conflict. The classical analysts' interpretations were directed toward pointing out the specific defenses being used and at a level that could be comprehended by a mature observing ego. The following classical interpretations exemplify this point;

"The tailor represents me, the analyst, whom you depreciate and make dark-skinned like your mother." In this interpretation, the conflict is between inferiority and superiority. The patient displaces his sense of inferiority and projects onto the analyst, the tailor, who becomes the depreciated on.

Another example: "When you find yourself wanting something from someone, you have a tendency to deny that that person might have something to give, and even turn it around so that he or she needs you. You want to be needed, rather than the other way around." The analyst here alludes to the conflict between dependence and independence. The patient denies his neediness and acts as though others need him: he is the independent one. The defenses interpreted are repression and reaction formation.

Our raters agreed than Kernberg was also identifiable by the way he interpreted defense and resistance. They noted his tendency to point out the patient's devaluation and depreciation as a defense against his underlying rage and envy. Some noted the accent on projection, especially the projection of aggressive feelings as a defensive maneuver. They saw Kernberg as dealing with grandiosity as a defense against feeling humiliated (Kernberg, 1975). One noted that the devaluation of the analyst, in Kernberg's view, was a defense against feeling needy, which makes the patient feel depreciated. This, of course, is similar to the prototypic classical analyst's interpretation, which helps to clarify why many raters mistook Kernbergian interpretations for classical ones.

One of our raters (E. Shane) described her view of a typical Kernbergian interpretation as "the intricate weaving of object relations, defensive manifestations, displacement from current objects to analyst and from analyst to current objects." She cited as an example the interpretation of our Kernbergian analyst: "Your sense that if I knew that you felt hurt and rejected yesterday, it would be like arming me; this reflects your attributing to me a sense of superiority when you think you need me and, by the same token, a sense of humiliation on your part. You protect yourself against this sense of humiliation by depreciating the analytic session."

There was a consensus on the second variable, like the way in which the transference is interpreted, in the case of the Kohutian and the Kleinian analysts, both obtaining a score of 3. The transference interpretations of the Kohutian presented the analyst as concerned, caring, and empathic, as one who would rectify the patient's deficit pathology with his empathy and attunement (Kohut, 1977). One analyst described the Kohutian transference interpretations as having an overriding emphasis on object need and hunger. The negative transference, on the other hand, is ignored, the transference is seen in terms of positive self-object transferences (Kohut, 1984). Another rater noted in the Kohutian interpretations that transference seemed to be construed as a joining together, as a bonding experience. Any rupture is interpreted in order to soothe over a rift in the patient-analyst relationship. One rater suggested that we were remiss in not including a seventh dimension, "the subjective experience" to fully capture the self-psychological experience. However, it is our position that the focus on intersubjectivity in self-psychology is the unique focus in the transference relationship.

In the Kleinian's handling of transference, it was felt that the emphasis was on aggression and projection. Moreover, it was the primitive transference pattern that was interpreted. The patient was portrayed as depreciating and spoiling the analyst's good intentions. Interpretations repeatedly went to the genetic roots and focused on the archaic, primitive levels of psychic experience (Klein, 1957).

The third variable involved focus on the patient's vulnerability. Practically all the raters gave the Kleinian analyst a 0 rating, and the Kohutian analyst a rating of 3. When they explained their 0 rating for the Kleinian, most raters stated that he gave no consideration to the patient's vulnerability, that there was no apparent attention to the effect the analyst's interpretations might have on the sensibilities of the patient.

When they explained their rating of 3 for the Kohutian on the vulnerability variable, they noted the emphasis on healing the self, on the assumption that the patient suffered from a deficit pathology (Kohut, 1984). Some analysts felt there was almost an excessive the interest in the vulnerability of the patient, especially a vulnerability to disorganization. In fact, this was thought to be a central theme for the Kohutian analyst (Kohut, 1984).

The fourth variable concerned the focus on the patient's primitive impulses. Again, there was consensus with regard to the interpretations of the Kohutian and the Kleinian analysts, the Kleinian receiving a 3 score and the Kohutian receiving a 0 rating. With regard to the Kohutian's 0 rating, it was repeatedly stated that primitive impulses addressed, that this is not a focus of the Kohutian analyst. On the other hand, the raters explained their 3 rating for the Kleinian on primitive impulses by stating that primitive impulses are being constantly addressed, especially those of an oral, greedy nature. A. Goldberg (rater) suggested that the Kleinian appears to assume that "present manifestations in the material of the hour derive directly from homologous, intrapsychic experiences in the first months of life. Orality and anality predominate in the interpretations, and these interpretations go immediately to early genetic roots." He felt there was no concern for the extreme distance between the depth of the interpretation and the patient's ability to connect with the interpretation.

In relation to the fifth variable, the focus on the patient's hostility, there was also a consensus in relation to the Kohutian and the Kleinian analysts, the Kohutian scoring 0 and the Kleinian scoring 3. It was stated that the aggression and badness of the patient are emphasized in the Kleinian's interpretation, while the analyst tends to present himself as a fount of goodness. Many of the raters pointed out the accusatory nature of the Kleinian interpretations and the emphasis on the destructive envy of the patient.

All raters noted the lack of interpretations related to hostile aggressiveness in the Kohutian analysts. One rater (D. Siegel), however, suggested that hostile aggressiveness is recognized, although not mentioned, as a reaction to the underlying hurt and damage. In other words, aggression is understood as a reaction to empathic failure, so it is the latter that is interpreted.

The sixth and last variable, the use of catchwords or phraseology, again found the Kohutian and Kleinian analysts receiving a score of 3 as a consensual rating. With regard to the Kohutian analysts it was stated that there was an emphasis on healing, that the analyst used terms like "sturdier self," emphasizing the neediness of the patient, his vulnerability, his damage and his disappointment, his "deep wound." It was also noted that there was a "sweet tone" of togetherness and understanding in the Kohutian format, and the use of terms indicating that the analyst and patient were working together. In the case of the Kleinian, there was use of terminology that involved anatomical parts and bodily products: the breast, the penis, references to oral terms, referring to the analyst's interpretations as good, the use of anal terms, "shit" and "piss," the emphasis on part-objects, clearly identifying the Kleinian language.

An example of the way in which these prototypic analysts differed is reflected in the interpretations each gave to the patient's refusal to listen to the analyst's interpretation of his dream. The Kohutian's interpretation was: "My starting to speak about the dream made it appear to you that I was oblivious to the continuing effect upon you and our relationship, of the loss of your hour and my sending you away, of the deep wound you have sustained, and of the importance of some time and space for healing to take place so that the meaning of that experience might be investigated together." The Kleinian, on the other hand, interpreted the patient's refusal to listen to the analyst as follows: "You call our interpretations bits of shit, wrong and insignificant, whereas you treat your own words as if they were food for thought—like the breast, or something very exciting—seminal things like the penis, whereas in fact they are all banal and pretenses." The classical analyst interpreted: "You need to make what I am saying insignificant to you because, if it had any merit, you wouldn't be able to maintain the feeling that you are completely independent and superior to me. It's like your tailor. If you didn't feel completely superior, you might begin to worry that the tailor could hurt you in some way." The Kernbergian interpreted: "I think you devalue potential contributions I might make to the interpretation of your dream and, in fact, make your own attempt to analyze the dream."

How do we understand these differences? In the case of the Kohutian analyst, it would appear that he focuses on the rupture of the empathic tie rather than on the possibility that the patient may not have wanted to hear an interpretation of the murder dream. The focus on the importance of the relationship is stressed. Catchwords like "deep wound" and "space for healing" are mentioned, and again the bonding emphasis in the phrase "the meaning of that experience might be investigated together." In the Kleinian's interpretation, the patient receives "bits of shit" from the analyst, and treats his own ideas as "food for thought." It is clear that the analyst experiences the patient's words as an attack. The Kleinian catchwords are reflected in the use of the words "breast," "penis," and "shit," the characteristic reference to anality and to body parts. The classical analyst addresses himself to the resistance of the patient at a level at which the patient is functioning, in contrast to the Kleinian who interprets the patient's resistance as expressed through a primitive fantasy. The classical analyst interprets the patient's reaction as a transference to the tailor-analyst, and he appears to be speaking to the mature, observing ego of the patient. In the Kleinian interpretation, the analyst appeals to the primitive ego of the patient. When the self-psychologist speaks to the patient, he maintains his focus on the rupture in the relationship that occurred as a result of the missed session. Two of our raters noted in the classical analyst's interpretation a reference to the patient's underlying castration anxiety as a motive for the patient's stance of defensive superiority. It was pointed out that oedipal conflict and castration anxiety were not evident in the interpretations of the analysis in the other theoretical groups. In the Kernbergian interpretation, "I think you devalue potential contributions I might make to the interpretation of your dream . . . ," we note the tendency to focus on the patient's depreciation of the analyst to protect himself from his underlying rage and envy (Kernberg, 1975). Two of our raters commented that it is characteristic of Kernberg to use the word "devalue" in his interpretations (Kernberg, 1975). Yet, like the classical analyst, he seems to address his interpretation to the mature, observing ego of the patient and to the negative transference resistance. It should be more apparent now why many of our raters mistook Kernbergian interventions for classical ones.

Summary of Findings

We have attempted to integrate our findings by presenting a composite portrait of each of the prototypic analysts from our four theoretical groups. This includes not only the consensual material, but also some of the insightful observations of one or another of our select group of raters. The Kleinian provided the most clear-cut recognizable pattern of intervention. It appears that his language was an immediate clue to his identity—the reference to sexual anatomical parts: penis, breast; the use of anal and oral terms: "shit," "piece of shit," "shitty person," "food for thought," "stools coming from your bottom are all equated with the breast." The emphasis in his interpretations is on the aggression and badness in the patient, who depreciates the goodness of the analyst. The interpretations also refer immediately to the early genetic roots, There is no reference to the recent event that may have triggered the patient's upset, namely, the fact that the patient missed the previous session due to an error on his part. The Kleinian actively intervenes, giving twice as many interpretations as analysts identified with the other three theoretical models. While this study cannot draw any conclusions about the effect this may have, the frequency of interventions is clearly a distinguishing feature of the Kleinian approach in treatment. It was also noted that the Kleinian gave more detailed and more primitive interpretations of the dream material. Raters from the other three groups claim to refrain from interpreting a dream extensively when there is a relative lack of associations and gave this explanation as to why the analysis from the other three perspectives did not interpret the dream as the Kleinian did. Perhaps the Kleinian's dream interpretations are in keeping with his relative alacrity in interpreting more primitive, archaic levels of the psyche.

The Kohutian, like the Kleinian, has his special style of intervening and his special language to express his conceptual schema. The theoretical stance that views the patient as suffering from empathic failure, from damaged self-esteem, from deficient self-esteem, from deficient self-self-object ties (Stolorow and Lachmann, 1980; Kohut, 1984), is conveyed in phrases like "increased vulnerability," "helpless vulnerability," deep wound," "the hope to acquire a sturdier self." The Kohutian makes a repeated effort to preserve the bonding, the togetherness, the connectedness between the patient and the analyst. This effort is also reflected in the Kohutian's phraseology. The following are excerpts from his interpretations: 1) "the importance of the experience is clear as well as our need to understand it"; 2) "You have an intensified need to be assured of my continued interest in you"; 3) "You hope that this can be contained within our continuing relationship"; and 4) "The meaning of that experience might be investigated together." The focus is on the rupture of the bond and how to repair it. When the rupture occurs, the analyst tends to blame himself rather than the patient (Kohut, 1979). Recall the interpretation of the self-psychologist: "My starting to speak about the dream made it appear to you that I was oblivious of the continuing effect upon you and our relationship of the loss of your hour and my sending you away, of the deep wound you have sustained." Contrast this interpretation with the one made by the Kleinian at the same juncture: "You call our interpretation bits of shit, wrong, and insignificant, whereas you treat your own words as if they were food for thought—like the breast."

The classical analyst offered no clear-clear gestalt, as did the two preceding prototypic analysts, yet one can be discerned. The interpretations are clearly directed toward defense and resistance and at the surface, easily comprehended by a mature, observing ego (Fenichel, 1941; Greenson, 1967). The interpretations are sometimes couched in the form of questions or tentative suggestions, as if to elicit further thought and reflection on the part of the patient. Some of our raters have stated that these interpretations lack the conviction and forcefulness of the Kleinian and Kohutian analysts. Conflicts about masculinity and femininity are interpreted; this can be considered a reference to phallic, oedipal conflicts and castration anxiety (Brenner, 1982).

The following interpretation more than some of the other interpretations, the characteristics of a classical intervention: "You are unconsciously testing to see if I am concerned, that is, when I turn to somebody else and ignore you. In telling me the wrong week in which you would be absent, you were allowing yourself to risk feeling the same way with me that you felt with your mother, and later your father, namely, that I would turn to other people and ignore you. The temptation to desert me in response to feeling deserted must be great." This interpretation not only connects the transference with genetic roots, but specifies it in relation to the defenses that are used, like turning passive into active and identifying with the aggressor.

The prototypic Kernbergian is not clearly differentiated from the Classical analyst. He, too, interprets defense and resistance at the surface and within the transference. One notes, however, a greater focus on the interpretation of the negative transference. As already mentioned, certain raters identified Kernbergian interpretations through their reference to the patient's tendency to devalue the analyst as protection against feeling of humiliation and rage; Kernberg (1986, 1987) has emphasized in his writings the importance of helping the patient recognize his contradictory ego states. This seems to be exemplified in the interpretation: "You do not seem to have been aware of the intensity of your rage that you felt rejected when I did not see you on Monday. The fact that you were aware of being pissed off indicates that you perceived yourself as being thrown to, depreciated—in other words, treated in a way you tend to treat me at times."

In sum, our research study tends to confirm that the theoretical differences among the groups we have studied are quite real and that they are converted into differences in treatment approach. What difference do these differences make? That is a question for future researchers to answer. In the next chapter a study of the defense mechanisms of the four analytic theories will be described.

This study was published in 1990. The differences that differentiate each theoretical group in this paper still obtain today (2012). More recently there has been an emphasis in the literature on the outcome of the psychoanalytic treatment experience, referred to as therapeutic action; and several different theoretical perspectives have put forth their theoretical understanding of what makes for successful psychoanalytic treatment. This will be discussed in chapter 10.

Chapter Three

Protective Devices of the Human Psyche

This chapter examines the means by which the human psyche protects itself. Aware of the varying theoretical viewpoints about this subject matter, the study will be restricted to four psychoanalytic perspectives: classical, Kleinian, Kernbergian and self-psychological; and it will focus on the similarities and differences among these schools in their conceptualization of defensive strategies. The author proposes that no one theoretical base can adequately encompass the wide array of available defensive constellations, and therefore suggests the possibility of crossing theoretical boundaries to build a more comprehensive, inclusive picture of the psychic armamentarium.

> The art of life is the art of avoiding pain.
> —Thomas Jefferson

In recent years there has been a burgeoning of theory construction in psychoanalysis, and the emphasis has tended to be on the theoretical and clinical differences among the various analytic schools (Kernberg, 1996); however, in this paper I plan to examine common threads which link seemingly unrelated concepts embedded in different theoretical perspectives. More specifically I plan to focus on those concepts in the different psychoanalytic theories which purport to explain how we protect ourselves from psychic pain. What are the roots shared by different theoretical perspectives, masked by differences in terminology? What differences are fundamental? What are the similarities and differences in the interpretive approach to defensive barriers? And lastly, what difference do these differences make in clinical practice? I have selected the classical, Kleinian, self-psychological, and Kernbergian schools as my objects of study. I am well aware that many more exist; but to narrow the focus of the paper, I have omitted other theoretical perspectives, such as the relational and intersubjective models.

In underscoring the stated purpose of the chapter, I have stressed the importance of understanding how the four schools conceptualized their differences and similarities with regard to defensive strategies. These differences and similarities will be examined along three dimensions: 1) the form and function of defenses, 2) developmental schemas (i.e., how, when and why protective devices are formed), and 3) the interpretative approach to defense.

Form and Function

The four models of the mind I have chosen have all conceptualized psychic structures and processes which provide protection against psychic pain. They have all posited constellations of defenses that have adaptive, as well as pathological, implications. Nevertheless, it is difficult to present a definition of defense broad enough and inclusive enough that all groups would subscribe to it. Gerald Aronson (personal communication) provided a definition that he believes all four groups would accept. It is a definition that was evolved out of the function of defense. The function of defense according to Aronson is "to arrange or to re-arrange mental content to prevent or lessen and/or stabilize and/or master psychic pain."

The classical school has incorporated the adaptive point of view as an integral part of its metapsychology, and this is exemplified by the functions it has assigned to some of the defense mechanisms it postulates; for example, regression can be adaptive and useful in certain situations, particularly creative ones (A. Freud, 1936). It has been termed regression in the service of the ego. Repression is considered an essential mechanism in development. Reaction formation is an aid in character formation. Sublimation has a very special position in the sense that it can be considered a displacement to higher aims as a way of resolving conflict. Identification with the aggressor is thought to be very important in the mastery of trauma and in superego formation. All the mechanisms of defense in the classical frame appear in normal development (A. Freud, 1965).

The Kleinian school has also examined the adaptive nature of defense (H. Segal, 1963). Projective identification is viewed as the earliest form of empathy. It involves the capacity to put oneself in another person's shoes. According to Kleinian theory, it also reflects the earliest form of symbol formation by projecting parts of oneself into the object and identifying parts of the object with parts of the self. These become the ego's first primitive symbols. Idealization contains a belief in the goodness of objects. Hanna Segal points out that it comes into play later in life when an individual falls in love, or appreciates beauty, or develops social or political ideals. The manic defense, characterized by control, triumph, and contempt, defends against depressive feelings and feelings of loss and guilt. In fact, the Kleinian concept of manic reparation is one in which the aim is to repair the object so that loss and guilt are not experienced.

Kernberg recognizes—particularly in the case of narcissistic personality disorders—that certain adaptive defenses operate so that good social functioning is possible, together with adequate impulse control and the potential for what Kernberg (1984) terms "pseudo-sublimation." He points out that such individuals retain the capacity to engage in activities that allow them to at least partially fulfill their ambitions of greatness, and in this way, are able to obtain admiration from others; indeed, they may be quite creative in their fields as their adaptive defenses allow them to use their creativity. According to Kernberg, the integrated, although highly pathological grandiose self, helps to compensate for the lack of integration of the normal self-concept. Kernberg believes that this formulation helps to explain the paradox of relatively good ego functioning and surface adaptation in the presence of a predominance of splitting mechanisms, primitive defenses, and a lack of integration of object representations.

The adaptive aspect of defensive operations in the self-psychological school are probably best viewed as protective devices that shore up or compensate for a defective self. For example, the mirroring and grandiose self-objects help to stave off feelings of inadequacy and worthlessness. As Segal (1996) states, "[T]he self-object . . . (is) . . . an object that acts as a component of the self in a way that supports and facilitates growth." The two types of structures that Kohut (1977) postulated, namely defensive and compensatory, are secondary structures formed to cope with the traumatization of a child's emerging self. They attempt to cover over the defects in the self.

In all four schools the recognition of the adaptive nature of the psyche's protective devices sounds a cautionary note: a patient's mental armamentarium should not be tampered with without careful consideration and understanding of the patient's need for such protection.

Developmental Schemas—How, When, and Why Protective Devices Are Formed

Why are such defensive measures necessary in the psychological development of human beings? And how do they evolve? Certainly our long dependency period is a major contributing factor. If we emerged fully grown, empowered with maturity, wisdom, physical power, the ability to perceive and accept reality, along with equanimity in the face of uncertainty, in the best of all possible worlds, self-deceptive devices might not be necessary. We could face reality, take our "lumps" and carry on, without resorting to deceiving ourselves. But we develop slowly, dependent on our caretakers, parental figures, to love us, protect us, nourish us, instill self-confidence and self esteem and help us to become civilized, as in tame any excessive expression of aggressivity or impulsivity. Parental care, however, is not always ideal or consistent; mothers and fathers can respond differently to their children depending on their own family experiences, as well as what idiosyncratic and bedrock problems the child might contribute. The world can become a frightening place, when for real or imagined reasons we become anxious either as children or adults. Our minds have the potential to conjure up ways of deceiving ourselves in the attempt to fashion a safe world and to escape from psychic pain. Unfortunately, this ability to protect ourselves does not always serve adaptive needs; the defenses erected can seriously interfere with our functioning and cause their own torment.

In an attempt to answer the questions raised in the previous paragraph, I will begin by examining some of the similarities and differences of the different schools as they relate to the normal and pathological development of psychic defenses. The reader at this point could logically object to the multiplicity of theories that attempt to explain the psychology of psychic defensiveness. It must be kept in mind that theory and practice in psychoanalysis are restricted by the subject matter: they deal primarily with subjective mental phenomena and must necessarily rely on hypothetical constructs to explain observable events. The very fact that the practice of psychoanalysis is dependent on inferred meanings of a patient's intrapsychic and interpersonal functioning necessitates working within a theoretical frame, while at the same time inviting the creation of alternative explanatory concepts. Psychoanalysis is different from other sciences in that the observations of the observer are more likely to introduce subjective and biased interpretations (Paniagua, 1995). Clearly, every way of seeing (i.e., theorizing) can be a way of not seeing, so that a given theoretical focus may well blind an analyst to recognizing and understanding certain mental phenomena, while in the process of highlighting others.

All the schools use some form of internalization as a construct in understanding how the psyche builds its armamentarium. In turn any discussion of internalization must necessarily include an internal object relations theory. I maintain that the four psychoanalytic theories under study do so. Although object relations theory is usually identified as a Kleinian formulation, the concept of an internal object was foreshadowed very early in Freud's writings. Sandler (1990) points out that when Breuer and Freud published *Studies on Hysteria* in 1895, "Freud had referred to transference as a 'false connection' between someone who had been the object of the patient's earlier wishes and the doctor now treating the patient. But in order to have such a 'false connection' between the past and the present, the object of the earlier wishes must have been internalized" (p. 860). Of course, there is also Freud's oft stated characterization of the ego as the "precipitate of abandoned object-cathexis" (S. Freud, 1923, p. 29). To quote Clifford Yorke (1994): "Freud was the first and only deviser of object-relations theory, and he gave us a way of regarding such relations which we would be wise not to ignore" (p. 382). Regarding the formation of the superego, Freud (1949) stated in *An Outline of Psychoanalysis*, "This new psychical agency continues to carry on the functions which have hitherto been performed by people (the abandoned objects) in the external world" (p. 20).

In the Kleinian school the concept of internal objects is central to understanding their theory of defense (Klein, 1946, 1955, 1957). While introjections are based on parental objects developing from bodily parts to whole objects, these internalized objects are never exact duplicates of the real parents, but rather influenced by the infant's instinctually driven fantasies and projections. The defenses upon which Klein focused evolved from the earliest stages of life. In fact, her primitive defenses such as splitting, idealization, projective identification, and omnipotence were thought to come into action during the paranoid-schizoid position, as in the first three months of life.

Projective identification has increasingly been considered a useful construct and not only among Kleinians but in the other analytic schools as well (Gabbard, 1994). Spillius (1992) describes this mechanism in simple and clearly understood terms: ". . . the most basic and primitive anxiety of the paranoid-schizoid position is a fear of annihilation from within the personality and that in order to survive, the individual projects this fear into external object as a defensive measure. This makes the external object bad, and the object is then likely to be attacked. Often the idea of the external object, somewhat distorted by projection, gets taken inside the personality and the infant (patient) feels that he is being attacked by an internal persecutor" (p. 60).

Splitting protects and preserves the good object by splitting off the hostile or bad aspects of the object. It is important to note that defenses in Kleinian theory often take the form of fantasies which attempt to fulfill instinctual drives. For example, these fantasies may provide a defense against the external reality of deprivation, as well as a defense against internal reality, such as the individual's own hunger and anger. According to Kleinian theory, fantasies can also be used as defenses against other fantasies. For example, manic defenses are commonly found to defend against depressive fantasies. In normal development, in accordance with the Kleinian schema, the schizoid and paranoid trends have largely subsided when the depressive period begins. It is then possible for the ego to use repression as a defense mechanism. In the paranoid-schizoid position, defenses are not only a means to protect the ego from immediate and overwhelming anxiety, but also are considered stepping stones in development which lead to the integration achieved in the depressive position.

Kernberg (1979, 1984) too has also incorporated the concept of internal objects as crucial to understanding the development of defensive organization, although he has rejected Klein's ideas about the earliest expressions of fantasies involving part objects. His etiological timetable is more in line with the traditional classical developmental stages. It is clear that he has drawn from both object relations theory and classical ego psychology when he evolved his formulations regarding defense. He views unconscious intrapsychic conflict not as simply conflict between impulse and defense, but conflict between two opposing sets of internalized object relations. Each set consists of a self and an object representation affected by a drive derivative, which is experienced as an affect.

In Kernberg's theoretical schema borderline patients use the more primitive defenses like splitting, projective identification, denial, omnipotence, or devaluation. He terms them lower-level defenses and states that they are present early in life. He considered splitting the major defensive process that keeps apart the mental representation of the good and bad self and objects. Here we see the similarity to Klein's thinking. Even denial in its primitive form is viewed by Kernberg as a form of splitting. To quote Kernberg (1975): "Denial, then, is a broad group of defensive operations and probably related, at its higher level, to the mechanisms of isolation and other higher-level defenses against affects (detachments, denial in fantasy, denial in word and act) and, at its lower level, to splitting" (p. 32).

Kohut introduced the concept of self-object into self-psychological theory. Although he did not specifically designate self-objects as serving defensive functions, it would seem that they do. They develop, according to self-psychological theory, primarily because of inadequate parental mirroring and/or the absence of a good-enough idealized parental object. A mirroring self-object presumably helps to stave off feelings of inadequacy and worthlessness. An idealized self-object creates the illusion of being protected by a powerful parental figure. A self-object has been defined as an object experienced as part of the self—an external object that services certain self-preservative needs not met by significant caretakers. I suggest that its building blocks consist of some form of internalization, splitting, projection of an ideal object, regression, denial, and negation.

The definition of self-object, incidentally, is reminiscent of Fenichel's description of the oral character, dependent on objects for the maintenance of self-esteem—the age-appropriate range being the first year of life in the classical schema. Fenichel (1945) noted that such individuals need external supplies to provide narcissistic gratification and the like to bolster their feelings of self-esteem.

The self-psychological concept of transmuting internalization is another case in point. In the self-psychological schema, it occurs when there is optimal frustration that allows for the conversion of self-object transferences into self structure. It seems to me that there is a parallel between transmuting internalization and the classical concepts of identification and identification with the aggressor which, in turn, can be viewed as part of the defensive armamentarium that are converted into self structure.

I would also like to raise the question as to whether the Kleinians and self-psychologists are dealing with the same mental phenomena in the Kleinian concept of projective identification and the self-psychological concept of self-object. Each construct hypothesizes an internalization of an object over which one needs to exert control and which provides some measure of psychic comfort and protection. Might the forerunner of this process be contained in the classical concept of object cathexis and in the defense mechanism of projection? In the search for commonalities that bind the four theories, the concept of self-objects could be considered a type of projective identification, as postulated by Kleinians, because it uses both projection and internalization in its formation.

I suggest that the four theories under study posit that an internalization process aids in developing the protective devices of the mind. Where defenses are triggered by the superego or the ego ideal, they are built upon internalization. For example, there is no reaction formation without an identification with a parental attitude as a precondition; hence, internalization is clearly a necessary forerunner of the development in this particular protective device. Moreover, in other protective devices as well, internalization of parental and cultural attitudes is the building block that dictates what must be warded off and how it is to be done. It follows that the defenses against the moral affects, such as guilt, humiliation and shame, ward off what can be considered the product of internalization. Boesky in a 1983 paper stressed that internalization and identification are concepts essential to understanding normal and pathological psychic structure formations. "These self- and object representations have become the individual bricks of the (psychoanalytic) theoretical system, and the entire inverted pyramid of theory rests on the single point of a solitary basic concept: the mental representation" (p. 565).

The importance of internalization across theoretical boundaries is also reflected in the classical concept of object constancy as described by Mahler (1968), the Kleinian idea that internalized objects are unconscious fantasies that keep the object constantly inside, and the Kernbergian proposition that splitting allows for the preservation of the good object and therefore the availability of the good object. In self-psychology, if the mirroring and/or grandiose transferences and the need for self-objects are analyzed according to self-psychological principles, the analysis will result in a transmuting internalization and in turn a healthy cohesive self; again the concept of internalization is crucial in theory construction.

Variations in Developmental Timing

Each school has postulated different timetables for the emergence of different defenses, as well as emphasizing some more than others. In the classical school it is proposed that a child has to achieve a distinction between ego and id before repression can be used as a mechanism; nor is sublimation available as a protective device in the very early years. Sublimation is considered dependent on the existence of certain superego values; therefore repression and sublimation are not in evidence until later in development. On the other hand, it was thought that regression, reversal, and turning against the self were not related to a particular stage of development and therefore they might well be used by the ego earlier. A. Freud (1965) considered introjection and projection closer to the id than other defense mechanisms, and, therefore, closer to the primary process when they were not defensive. Yet she further stated that these mechanisms may serve defensive purposes when used by the ego. Apparently what she meant was before these defenses can be used, there has to be a distinction between inner and outer worlds; that is, there are preconditions that lay the foundation for the establishment of this distinction. Higher forms of projection clearly require a differentiation between the inner and outer world, because, if there is no outer world, it is not possible to project anything onto it. Also essential to understanding the classical point of view is the premise that conflict facilitates development, while it also mobilizes defenses.

In any consideration of Klein's theoretical conceptualization of the development of defenses, it must be understood that the ego in Kleinian theory exists from birth and, therefore, it uses defenses of a primitive nature from the very beginning of life; but there is a hierarchical ordering in terms of the appearance of these defenses in accordance with stage appropriateness. The defenses of splitting, idealization, denial, omnipotence, projection, introjection, and projective identification all come into operation by the age of three months during the paranoid-schizoid position. Klein specifically stated that the failure to overcome their use would not only interfere with the child's attaining the depressive position, but would result in these defenses being used throughout life. Klein stressed that it is necessary to identify with the good object, as it brings with it the feeling that one possesses goodness of one's own. The failure of the infant to identify with the good object leads to the development of pathological defenses. Clearly, the importance of internalized object relations is apparent in Klein's formulation of the defensive organization. Most important to keep in mind is that the Kleinian timetable for its developmental stages is condensed into a very early period of infant development and does not correlate with the classical stages of ego development (Klein, 1946, 1955, 1957).

Kernberg's view of development is closely tied in with the classical frame with its Mahlerian additions to the understanding of early maturational stages (Kernberg, 1984).

During the latter part of the first year and into the second year, in accordance with Kernberg's timetable, splitting functions as a defense to ward off hostility toward the object and to protect the positive introjections and identifications. Kernberg suggests that in borderline patients, these primitive defenses continue to be used because of ego weakness and, indeed, contribute to this ego weakness. Children who are healthy are less likely to use primitive defenses. Instead, the child begins to use higher-level defenses such as repression, reaction formation, displacement, and isolation.

Kernberg (1975) states his developmental view in this quote: "One essential task in the development and integration of the ego is the synthesis of early and later introjections and identifications into a stable ego identity" (p. 20). However he points out that the initial inability of the infant to effect such an integration is used defensively by the ego via the mechanism of splitting, in order to avoid being overwhelmed by anxiety, and to protect the ego built on positive introjections. According to Kernberg, splitting is usually effective during the first year of life. It is then replaced by what he terms "higher-level defensive operations of the ego": repression, reaction formation, isolation, and undoing. Unlike Klein who telescopes development into the first year of life, Kernberg thinks that the formation of the psychic structure takes place in the first three years.

Kohut's developmental schema, as it relates to defenses, is drawn with broad brushstrokes in contrast in the other theoretical perspectives. Kohut (1977) conceptualizes defensive organization that allows the child to be protected from the traumatization of his/her emerging self. It leads to the formation of two types of structures which were described earlier, namely, defensive structures and compensatory structures. These structures develop in relation to the flaws, or defects, acquired. The flaws are termed primary defects and are experienced as feelings of worthlessness, depression, emptiness, and loneliness, due primarily to inadequate parental mirroring. The two types of structures, defensive and compensatory, are secondary structures formed to cope with the primary defect.

Kohut's emphasis on the deficits and flaws in the child's developmental experience contrasts with the classical view which focuses on the conflicts that the child must resolve at each developmental stage. For example, the self-psychologist's view of the oedipal period is that it is only conflictual if there has been an earlier developmental failure, or deficit, rather than the classical view that oedipal conflict is ubiquitous, ultimately leading to the formation of the mature superego. Self-psychology posits that optimal frustration, based on empathic failures of a non-traumatic nature, can lead to positive structural change via an internalization process.

This cursory review has tended to highlight the conceptual differences among the groups, and in part these differences are a function of the type of pathology each has chosen to study, as well as a different understanding of that pathology. For example, Klein's tendency to view defenses as warding off a regression due to the anxiety stirred by earlier danger situations gives a distinctive theoretical understanding of the obsessive-compulsive character disorder. This deviates from the classical view of the obsessive character formation, which posits a regression to the anal level due to the anxieties evoked by entering the oedipal phase.

Kernberg's major contribution lies in the specification of defense constellations which typify the borderline and narcissistic states. Self-psychological theory evolved out of the study of the narcissistic personality disorder. It has since broadened into a more general psychology, providing the basis for the treatment of a wide range of mental disorders. Nevertheless, the defensive strategies it has described primarily protect against extreme vulnerability to failure, disappointments, and slights. Both Kernberg and Kohut use the concept of the grandiose self as a defensive structure, but they conceptualize this construct quite differently. Kohut's view is that the conceptual origin of the grandiose self lies in the fixation of an archaic, "normal," primitive self; whereas Kernberg views it as a pathological structure clearly different from normal infantile narcissism.

There is another significant difference between self-psychology, on the one hand, and classical, Kleinian, and Kernbergian theories on the other that should be noted: The latter have incorporated instinct theory as explanatory in understanding why defenses had to be erected; they viewed defenses as unconscious strategies that people characteristically use to ward off instinctual drive derivatives, as well as painful memories, and unendurable ideas or affects. Kohut, on the other hand, minimized, and even negated, the significance of instinct. Kohut preferred to think of the defensiveness of patients and to think of their defensive attitudes within the framework of the analyst's overall understanding of the needs of the patient's self. The question that should be posed now is what difference do these differences make? And, in this paper, the arena where the answers will be sought is in the clinical sphere.

The Interpretative Approach to Defense

In the study described in chapter 2, we used clinical data drawn from the analysis of a 28-year-old male to examine the divergence in treatment approach in the four models under study. In this research project, we were able to determine at a highly significant statistical level that analysts could be distinguished as belonging to one of these four groups on the basis of the kind of interpretations they gave to a detailed written account of an analytic hour. As noted in the previous chapter, we examined six variables derived from a consensus of raters, who identified these factors as making it possible for them to make correct identifications. These factors dealt with 1) the manner in which defense and resistance were interpreted; 2) the way in which the transference was interpreted; 3) the focus on the patient's vulnerability; 4) the focus on the patient's primitive impulses; 5) the focus on the patient's hostile aggressiveness; and 6) the use of special catchwords or phraseology.

In retrospect all these variables relate on some level to the psyche's protective devices. Transference, for example, serves defensive purposes, even though it is not usually described as doing so. When transference is understood in part as an attempt to master the distressing aspects of significant early relationships in hopes of obtaining a different outcome or warding off the pain of separation from early objects, it clearly can be categorized as a protective device. Inderbitzin and Levy (1994) have described transference as a defense. "Transference creates a current interpersonal reality to defend against awareness of troublesome internal wishes and fears" (p. 772). While acknowledging transference as a displacement, they also point out: "Sometimes, in addition to the displacement, a reversal takes place, so that the impulses and feelings experienced and expressed toward the analyst are the opposite of those originally experienced toward important figures in childhood" (p. 772). This brings to mind Greenson's paper (1954), "The Struggle Against Identification," which might explain why the reversal takes place. I suggest that all four schools would in some form subscribe to these conceptualizations. To paraphrase Wallerstein, transference is a unifying concept that turns many psychoanalytic theories into one.

A patient's vulnerability, the way in which he expresses or inhibits his primitive impulses and/or aggressivity, all involve and evoke defensive maneuvers. Moreover, interdigitating theories as they relate to defense are complicated when different analytic schools use the same terminology to express essentially different constructs and different theoretical language to refer to the same or at least similar mental phenomena.

Although the study we conducted was published in 1990, the data were collected in the early and middle 1980s. Our subjects were selected primarily because they were recognized in their clinical work as representing one of the four points of view being studied, and indeed they identified themselves as belonging to one of these four analytic schools. However, while admittedly I do not have research data to substantiate my conclusion, I believe marked changes have occurred in clinical practice since our study was concluded, particularly in the way defense is interpreted. In the Kleinian school, for example, Spillius has noted that far fewer interpretations are directed toward the patient's destructiveness and indexes of the death instinct, and the language of interpretation is not likely to use the primitive body parts. To quote

Spillius (1988): "the general tendency . . . is to talk to the patient . . . less in terms of anatomical structures (breast, penis), and more in terms of psychological functions . . ." (p. 8). To me this suggests a greater sensitivity to the protective structures the human psyche erects because it is recognized there is a conflict over being in touch with such primitive unconscious material.

Klein believed defenses were expressions of unconscious fantasies and as such they were manifestations of instinct. She used direct and confrontational interpretations of this unconscious material. With the shift in the form of interpretation, modern Kleinians would appear to have incorporated a more classical or Freudian approach to the interpretation of defense. By the same token, as the Kleinians broadened their definition of countertransference to include the analyst's emotional reactions to the patient in order to gain a better understanding of the patient, it was viewed as a very useful tool by many classical analysts, self-psychologists, and, of course, Kernberg as well (Kernberg, 1987; Gabbard, 1994). The concept of projective identification, as discussed earlier, has been incorporated in one form or another in all four schools. It is also important to note that Kohut's emphasis on empathy has undoubtedly sensitized analysts of all persuasions to the fragility of patients; it has underscored the importance of attunement and monitored a more cautious and introspective approach to interpretative intervention.

Increasingly I believe the different schools have assimilated interpretive insights and approaches from each other; and while maintaining their theoretical orientation and identity, analysts in their clinical practice are blending different psychoanalytic perspectives in their interpretations, especially as they pertain to the defensive structures of their patients. The question arises, of course, as to whether it is possible to integrate the four theories into one. Certainly each body of theory has made its special contribution to understanding psychological development in general and, more specifically, to understanding the way in which the psyche protects itself from painful awareness.

I do believe that classical psychoanalytic theory has probably provided the broadest, most inclusive framework; whereas Kohut has deepened our understanding of the narcissistic personality, its development, and its treatment through his descriptions of the grandiose and mirroring transferences and his highlighting the importance of relating to the patient exclusively through his subjectivity. The Kleinians have certainly increased our understanding of the primitive dark side of man's nature—his greed, envy, and destructive impulses—and sharpened our awareness of primitive mechanisms of defense, like splitting and projective identification. Kernberg has broadened our understanding of object relations with his conceptualization of contradictory ego states, brought about by the conflict between two opposing sets of self and object representation.

Pine (1988) evolved a four-part schema to conceptualize the development and functioning of the human psyche that lead to stabilized character formation. Each of his four models, or psychologies as he terms them, purportedly cover the phenomena of mental life, in varying hierarchical order. They are the psychology of drive, the psychology of ego, the psychology of object relations, and the psychology of self. The dominant psychology is governed by what Pine terms a principle of moments: for example, sometimes self-experience is in the foreground and sometimes the experience that emanates from drives predominates.

Hanly (1994) believes, as I tend to do, that classical psychoanalytic theory contains the basis for the integration of multiple model theories like the one proposed by Pine. Hanly claims Pine's theoretical constellation fails to provide an interrelated dynamic view of causalities. He maintains that classical theory sidesteps this disadvantage, because it is more unified. Although Pine attempts in essence to integrate self-psychology and object relations theory with id psychology, Hanly holds that Pine fails to do so. Hanly prefers to rely on the hypothesis of psychic over determination as an explanatory concept; he insists that it is detrimental to clinical understanding to separate the dynamically interconnected psychic forces into four psychologies.

I have attempted in this paper to point out certain similarities across schools, sometimes disguised by language and conceptual emphasis of a particular school, as well as to ferret out substantive differences. My discussion has also focused on a consideration of integrating and using useful concepts in analytic work with patients that have been drawn from multiple analytic models. I believe that this is an important consideration. For that reason, I will now describe a case from my practice to illustrate those times when I believe my clinical understanding reflects the influence of one or another of the four analytic perspectives I have studied, specifically: as they pertain to the protective devices of the patient's psyche.

A Clinical Example

I have chosen a clinical vignette to support my thesis that many of the protective devices described by the four theoretical perspectives under study can be detected in a given analytic case. If such cross-fertilization can be demonstrated, it seems reasonable to postulate that these psychic armaments can fit into a unifying frame in psychoanalysis.

I will present the case of Denise, a woman in her forties who sought treatment because of intense feelings of loneliness. My first impression of Denise was that she was attractive, statuesque, and carried herself with considerable poise and dignity; yet at the outset of the analysis she complained of feeling awkward with people, always concerned that they might disapprove of her. In our first meetings she had a somewhat proper, pristine, contained manner; her dress was very conservative. During the period I have seen her, there has been a dramatic change in her manner and her dress. She is now usually spontaneous and outgoing and dresses in fashionable and even what one might describe as youthful seductive clothing.

Denise appears to be very competent in her professional work, enjoys it, and takes pride in her standards of excellence. She apparently has had fairly good relationships with her coworkers, although they are sometimes marred by her sensitivity to slights and rejection.

Her primary initial complaint concerned an overpowering need to feel loved, experienced as insatiable at times, as if she could never be "filled up." She would have rageful, uncontrolled outbursts if she felt these needs were not met, or she might withdraw emotionally from people at such times and turn to what she described as her "temple within," from which she would derive a sense of spirituality and superiority.

This patient was married when she began her analysis, but complained bitterly about her relationship with her husband, who traveled without her quite often and when present, according to the patient, was emotionally distant. About four months into the analysis, the husband asked for a divorce. Denise was devastated by his request. She had two previously failed marriages.

When I asked her in one of our first sessions what kept her in the marriage, she told me that she would get great comfort sitting on her husband's lap; he would put his arms around her, rock her, and cuddle her. "I feel my battery is run down and I have no interest in anything; but when my husband cradles me, I have a tongue reflex like a baby when it nurses; then my battery is restored."

A classical analyst might interpret this behavior as a regression to orality. A self-psychologist might attribute it to a need to make up for a lack of adequate parental mirroring in this patient's earlier years. As indicated earlier, there is kinship between this formulation and a classical analyst's description of the oral character, dependent on objects in order to maintain self-esteem. The Kleinian may speak in more primitive terms and describe this patient as a greedy baby in a desperate search for the good breast; but I suspect he too would consider that some crucial wounding had occurred in the first years of life. All would recognize that there were serious preoedipal problems to consider.

I do not negate the fact that there are substantive differences in the explanatory conceptualizations of the analytic theories under study; the classical analyst might be attuned more to the instinctual contributions to this patient's behavior—the rageful reactions and orality may be seen in part as indicative of powerful aggressive and sexual drives and perhaps a regressive defense to escape an oedipal conflict. Perhaps the Kleinian might even invoke the death instinct, and place greater emphasis on primitive unconscious fantasy. Kernberg's view would probably fall midway between the two; and, the self-psychologist would possibly focus on the absence of adequate self-objects and describe the angry outbursts as narcissistic rage in reaction to defective parenting. In the clinical setting I suspect all would examine the transference for signs of an early disturbance in the pre-oedipal mother-infant relationship.

Denise described her mother as a very compulsive woman, more concerned about keeping her home clean and tidy than being nurturing to her children. Denise said that she felt much closer and loving toward her father, despite the fact that he would have rageful outbursts and beat her with a belt, not to mention once he started the beatings, he had difficulty in stopping.

Denise has a younger sister who she felt was the mother's favorite because she was blonde, fairer in complexion and prettier. The sibling rivalry and desire to have her mother all to herself was played out in the transference: she became very upset when a friend she described as unusually beautiful wanted to seek treatment from me. It follows then that not only did Denise engage in sibling rivalry with certain peers, but she would be very preoccupied with her external appearance (e.g., she has subjected herself to various forms of cosmetic surgeries, silicone injection, and a facial peel). Interestingly enough, Denise's concept of beauty is based largely on her memory of her sister's appearance as a young child; so she has bleached her skin and her hair to effect this look. A self-psychologist might interpret these efforts as an attempt to ward off the narcissistic injury she sustained when she thought her mother preferred her younger, more beautiful sibling. Indeed, today Denise takes pride in looking younger and more beautiful than her sister, although when depressed, she has thought of herself as "ugly." These cosmetic devices also aided in staving off the effects of aging, also of great concern to this patient. I suspect analysts from the other analytic persuasions would concur that this family dynamic contributed to Denise's psychic wounding.

At this writing Denise has been in analysis four years. She has exhibited a wide range of defensive maneuvers to stave off psychic pain. The first year and a half of treatment was characterized by rather persistent resistance to acknowledging transferential reactions; this seemed to be an attempt to protect herself from caring about me for fear I might be critical or rejecting of her. As this resistance to the transference lessened, this fear would turn into rage when she was convinced that I, like her mother, was critically judging her.

After she would express hostility toward me, she would usually attempt to placate me in some manner: she would affirm how much I have helped her and how much our relationship has meant to her. I would then witness a striking reversal of affect. I interpreted this as her way of staving off her fear of loss and abandonment. Kernberg and Klein would note the use of splitting, probably as a way of preserving her relationship with me in the role of the good object. A classical analyst might view this as an example of reducing guilt through the mechanisms of undoing and reaction formation.

For about three years Denise has had an on-again off-again relationship with a man ten or twelve years younger than she is. There is a strong possibility he is bisexual, for he often associates with homosexual men, and has performed for them as a male dancer. Despite his primarily seeking out Denise when he wanted sex and rejecting her in a cruel, hostile manner when he satisfied his sexual needs, Denise repeatedly used denial to maintain the illusion that he loved her, that he was a caring person and could be the life partner she was seeking. When he would reject her in a hostile way, at first Denise would be enraged, then depressed and withdrawn. Suddenly the depression would appear to lift, and Denise became somewhat grandiose, overly cheerful and very seductive in her attempt to find other lovers.

From the Kleinian point of view, it appeared that she protected herself from her feelings of loss and depression at times by a form of manic denial. The classical analyst too would likely recognize this defense as denial in fantasy. When the depreciating, rejecting boyfriend sought her out again, Denise seemed to have erased from her mind his previous acts of cruelty and only his charm, his physical beauty, his in-the-moment devotion to her would take center stage in her awareness. Kernberg's concept of contradiction of self and object would also seem to shed light on her shifting perceptions of her lover and her way of relating to him. She would either experience him as a devoted caring partner or the devil incarnate; and she would perceive herself alternately as a princess with superior attributes or a pathetic, helpless victim of deceit and cruelty. There is clinical evidence that she was reenacting with this boyfriend her relationship with her abusive father, using defenses to hold on to that alternating brutal and loving relationship.

These contradictory self and object states (Kernberg) have been reflected in the transference as well—for a period I would be experienced as the loving wished-for mother who takes great pride in Denise's beauty and intelligence (a mirroring self-object: Kohut) or I was a witch who was offensive and critical of her (use of splitting and a projection of an internalized bad object, i.e., projective identification: Klein.) A self-psychologist would probably diagnose the patient as having a narcissistic personality disorder, given her marked vacillation between grandiosity and lack of self-worth; whereas, a Kleinian might view her as caught somewhere between the paranoid-schizoid and depressive positions. A classical analyst might emphasize her hysterical features as in the orality and the apparent Oedipal dynamic. I believe that it is instructive in line with the purpose of this paper to demonstrate how this patient uses strategies conceptualized by more than analytic schools.

As mentioned earlier Denise described her relationship with her father as a close, loving one; she deeply resented any attempt on her mother's part to intrude on this relationship. During the analysis Denise began to disabuse herself of this distorted illusory perception of her father, who both physically and verbally abused her. Three years into the analysis Denise decided to return to graduate school; she wanted to become a psychotherapist. Her profession up until this point was not remotely connected to the field of psychology and psychotherapy. This decision was based in part on an identification with me. She actually verbalized feeling she did not have an adequate role model in her mother and that I provided that for her; she said she had benefited from her analytic experience and she wanted to be helpful to others. She felt she had a special gift by virtue of her own sensitivity and insight and her psychological mindedness; therefore, she was able to understand and relate to troubled human beings.

She began to cite her textbook readings in a very didactic manner, as if to instruct me in psychodiagnostics and proper therapeutic techniques. If she experienced one of my interpretations as critical and judgmental, she would cite published authorities who would have interpreted the material differently. It also appeared that she hoped I would take pride and pleasure in her newly acquired knowledge. But also I sensed a competitive motive that would emerge in the negative transference: she would express contempt for Freudian theory and would depreciate my analytic interventions at such times. The Kleinians have emphasized that contempt protects one against feeling envy, and Denise's reaction seemed to exemplify this dynamic. She was particularly incensed by Freud's theory of the Oedipus complex. She thought it absurd to think children had any sexual feelings toward the parent of the opposite sex. Certainly she never harbored such thoughts.

I also recognized that she was lecturing me in a didactic manner the way she had described her father would lecture her, and I suspected she wanted me to feel inadequate and worthless the way she had felt with him at times. Here we note the protection that identification with the aggressor provides against feeling small and insignificant.

The negative transference, therefore, appeared to have some unresolved oedipal underpinnings. Denise believed I disapproved of her on again-off again relationship with Peter, the man ten or twelve years her junior. Her mother had been outspoken about her disapproval of this affair. In her sessions Denise tended to wait until the end of the session to mention that she had seen him, particularly if they had had sexual relations. There were also extratransferential manifestations: Denise has been very fond of her primary boss, Albert, and she sometimes used his wife, Naomi, as a confidante and a kind of mother figure. After I interpreted her withholding information about Peter until the end of the session because she thought I would be critical of her, she told me she was not aware of feeling this way, although it was probably true, because it occurred to her she did not plan to tell Naomi that she is seeing him, lest she disapprove.

The next session she reported the following dream near the end of the hour: "I was following Naomi and we ended up in a restaurant. I asked for the restroom, but I ended up outside. Pollen was coming down from the trees like they were crying. I went back to the restaurant building, but I couldn't find the door."

In her associations she said that sometimes Naomi is available, sometimes she is not. She never says goodbye on the weekends. (Naomi works in the same office as the patient.) But she admires her, especially because she has a good marriage and "in that respect, I'd like to follow her." When I suggested that there might be a connection between way she feels about Naomi and the way she feels about me, she said that there was something she had withheld from me—"the other night I ended up having intercourse with Peter. I didn't tell you. It happened in the bathroom." I said that she seemed to fear I would disapprove of her doing this. "In the dream, you follow Naomi into the restaurant to show you the way, but you lose her because you need to go to the bathroom. Like with Naomi who leaves you on weekends as I do, I suspect you fear you might lose me and be left out in the cold for good, because of carrying on with Peter in the bathroom. That might account for your waiting until the end of the hour to tell me this dream." Denise responded: "Yes, but I really didn't think of it when I came in here, so I wonder how many thoughts do I keep out of here?" In this instance Denise unconsciously used repression to preserve her relationship with me.

Her competitive oedipal strivings seemed to be reflected in the following dream and associations: "I was in a theater, like the Dorothy Chandler. It's a rehearsal. One of the actresses is Cher. She has a plan to kidnap the diva so she can do the final number. I caution her that the audience won't see the humor in it."

I asked her what came to mind about her objections to Cher's plan. She responded: "Cher's symbolic of me. Everyone said I looked like Cher when my hair was dark. I've been darkening it again."

"And the diva?" I asked. She responded: "My mom's always been the one on stage. She didn't stay in her generation. She didn't stay out. There wasn't space for me. She wanted to keep the kid in her place. As I moved into womanhood, she didn't want to move into the next stage. When my boyfriends came over, she would wear these low-cut dresses that showed her breasts, and she would flirt with them. So I remained the child." I said, "I suspect you have a conflict about wanting to take over your mother's role. In the dream you are in the audience, cautioning Cher that those observing you won't be amused by what you as Cher are trying to do."

"Yes," she noted, "that's a good observation. This weekend I thought, 'What does it take to be my age?' . . . I tremble at the idea of taking center stage." Then she told me a dream she had the same night: "It's also in a theater setting. I'm sitting with my cousin who is also my godmother. I say I love the theater but with my budget I can't go regularly. I wish they had a program on Saturdays where they sell vacant seats at low prices. Her response was rejecting: 'I'm not your mother!' Her look was disgusted. She walked over to my mother and said 'Get a load of her. She thinks I'm her mother. She's passing judgment.' I felt like I was being put down. I flicked her off. Fuck her!"

Her associations went to her mother. "My mother is hot and cold. She wants attention when she wants it. I don't get that mother likes me. When she wants to be mothered, she's there."

I said at this point: "In this last dream you want to go Saturday to the theater but at a bargain rate. What occurs to you about that?" Her response was: "My class on Saturday is about family therapy. I wish I could bring my family into family therapy, but I can't afford it. I wish I could."

I pointed out: "You can only afford analysis if the fee is reduced. And you missed your Friday appointment." (I had to attend a conference.) The patient laughed. "I wanted a Saturday session. But no, I was OK with your going away."

I said: "In the dream, your godmother-cousin rejects you, critical you might think of her as your mother. What occurs to you about that?" She responded: "I think that has to do with my Saturday class instructor. Last week I called her and asked for her e-mail address because I wanted to send her the paper I'm preparing for her class before I finished it, to get her input as to whether I was on the right track. She refused to give it to me and told me to work on the paper without special help from her. I was very hurt—I just was eager to learn, and she treated me like I was too needy—like I was looking for her to be my mommy, and she wanted none of it. This last Saturday, I didn't raise my hand to comment like I usually do. At the end of class I just walked out without saying good-bye to anyone."

Clearly she felt ashamed and demeaned by this incident and handled these feelings of humiliation by withdrawing. Denise denied having similar feelings about me, although in a recent analytic hour she had felt I was critical and depreciating of her when she had assumed I disapproved of her relationship with Peter. Given the proximity of the two dreams she reported, I thought that the fear of maternal disapproval and rejection interfered with her competitive strivings and created conflict in carrying out her wish to take her mother's place. I believe this fear tended to create a resistance, a protective wall, if you will, to getting in touch with her oedipal conflict.

This patient has contended that she only finds men sexually appealing if they are ten to twenty years her junior. She maintains that she prefers younger men because she feels and believes she looks much younger than her age. Moreover, she has claimed that she views herself as an innocent, and somehow sexual liaisons with younger men seem more innocent. From a self-psychological point of view, she protects herself from her defective sense of self equated with aging by seeking out grandiose self-objects in the form of handsome young "hunks."

The patient has described her aversion to men her age or older: she finds their grey hair and balding heads repulsive and cannot conceive being touched in any sensual way by them. She perceives them as lecherous, dirty old men. From the classical point of view she can be understood as staving off unacceptable oedipal fantasies, which awaken incestuous sexual longings. Kleinians might also perceive her invoking a form of projective identification. She projects onto the older men her own lascivious desires at the same time that her behavior is seductive with them. In this way she relieves herself of the responsibility of making any sexual advances toward them. However, because of a deeply ingrained need, contradicted by her outward behavior, to perceive herself as an innocent and a victim, she is disgusted by their response to her. In contrast she is aggressive in acting out her lustful fantasies with younger men, which in her internal world allow her to retain a childlike innocence. A classical analyst would probably recognize this sexually assertive behavior as a form of identification with the aggressor or turning passive into active.

In this chapter I have not provided the reader with a progressive portrait of this patient's analytic journey nor have I emphasized the gains she has achieved in her analytic work. However, I would like to note that currently Denise rarely resorts to the primitive splitting so prevalent at the beginning of her analysis. She has become increasingly psychologically minded and introspective. While she occasionally has rageful outbursts, she quickly recovers from them, she gains perspective, and she analyzes what she now considers an inappropriate reaction to the precipitating event. She feels she has made considerable gains in her treatment and reports that her friends of long standing often comment how different she is from the constrained, uptight, depressed person they had previously known.

The primary purpose in presenting this case has been to demonstrate how useful it can be to include in the analyst's toolbox a knowledge of a wide range of defensive strategies, as conceptualized by the four analytic schools under study. It would be well to heed Arlow's cautionary reminder (1995): "[W]e must be aware of the temptation to impose a favorite theory of pathogenesis as a paradigm upon the analysand's productions. . . . Otherwise, it is easy to be misled and pick and choose selectively from one's favorite paradigm . . . and discard the material that does not conform" (p. 216). With this admonition in mind, I maintain that one can cross theoretical boundaries and thereby build a cohesive composite portrait of a patient's psychic armamentarium. I believe that such a broadly based inclusive profile can provide an analyst with a more comprehensive understanding of the patient and hopefully enhance the analytic process.

The chapters that follow deal primarily with the psychoanalytically oriented treatment of children. The next chapter takes up the latency period, the six to twelve years age range.

Chapter Four

Latency

The psychoanalytic concept of the latency period originated with Freud. He introduced and defined it in 1905 as a phase in the sexual development of children. From then until the end of his life, Freud essentially maintained his initial view of latency and repeatedly stressed its importance in understanding normal and abnormal psychological development. He described the latency period as following the phallic-oedipal crest of infantile sexual development and extending until the onset of puberty. In 1926 (Inhibitions, Symptoms and Anxiety) he wrote that the latency period was "characterized by the dissolution of the Oedipus complex, the creation or consolidation of the superego and the erection of ethical and aesthetic barriers in the ego" (p. 114). He stressed the role of castration anxiety in bringing about repression and/or dissolution of the Oedipus complex and the increasing importance of guilt coming from the newly formed superego. He stated that instinctual breakthroughs do occur and that latency need not bring about an interruption of sexual interest.

The actual timing of the beginning and end of latency is difficult to determine and varies from child to child. We must factor in individual personality differences, family influences, and cultural patterns. But these variations do not invalidate the concept of latency. Latency represents a halt to the progression of infantile sexuality. Anna Freud (1936) stated that in the latency period all the defenses are in place and noted that fantasy was one of the defense mechanisms. The child's libidinal attachment to his parental love objects culminates in the Oedipus complex and is repressed with the onset of latency. Adolescence represents the second onset of sexual development, leading to genital maturity and libidinal investment in love objects outside the family.

Freud pointed out the important personality achievements during the latency period, especially the emergence of values, ideals, and sublimations, their positive implications for human cultural development. He also stressed, however, that the interruption in sexual development and repression of the oedipal complex can make man vulnerable to neurosis.

One of my psychotherapy patients, a man in his early thirties, sought treatment because he became so disinterested in, so repulsed by the idea of having any sexual contact with his wife that she threatened to leave him. He idealized those times when he was in elementary school, when he shone as a very bright student. He took great pride in being the good and the most accomplished child in his family. Unlike his rebellious brother, he did chores willingly and was his mother's favorite. He was polite and well mannered.

While in high school, he might take a girl to a prom, but he had no sexual interest in girls and felt rather superior to boys who did. There was some sexual awakening in college, although a couple of the women he went with complained he was not interested enough in being sexual. His primary interests were intellectual pursuits, but he added that he did enjoy a fast volleyball game "with the guys on the beach."

He had a powerful sense of right and wrong, and he was well mannered and considerate of others. He had a sexual affair with his wife before marriage. She tended to be more interested in being sexual than he. However, after they were married, his sexual interest tapered off and when his wife became pregnant, he lost all interest in being sexual and avoided it at all costs. When his wife issued her ultimatum, he did not want to lose her. Unfortunately, his motivation in seeking treatment was not that he wanted to change; rather he did not want his wife to leave him. He came to the point in the therapy when having sex with his wife no longer revolted him. He took a grin and bear it attitude and was agreeable to once-a-week intercourse. His wife no longer threatened to leave him. He then terminated his treatment.

While I think it is possible that constitutionally he was probably not endowed with a strong sexual drive, I am more inclined to think that the powerful repressive barriers erected in the latency period against his oedipal attachment had a far more potent effect. Both parents had a strong moral code that guided their child-rearing practices. Clearly this patient had formed a strict superego that warded off any incestuous desires and in turn dampened his sexuality. I thought it was significant that his total disinterest and even repulsion at the idea of having sex with his wife was when she became a mother.

Superego development is one of the crucial development achievements of the latency child. Anna Freud's work on the defenses, especially the defense of identification with the aggressor, provides an understanding of the intermediate stage in superego formation. The child can ward off the anxiety from psychic conflict by employing this defense, which is a combination of introjection, projection, and turning passive into active. Usually the newly formed superego tends to be harsh.

The latency child often engages me in games—Monopoly, Sorry, Life, the card game Uno—with an intense need to win. As the child transitions into late latency, the child often insists on rules and fairness, on the skill of playing as opposed to the thrill of winning, and on being competitive. This is the period that children love Harry Potter-type stories. How wonderful to believe in the magical power of wizard-children that masks their feelings of vulnerability and smallness and endows them with control over the threatening adults in their world. In the latency period, as in *Harry Potter*, good and evil are clear-cut and reflect the rudimentary beginnings of superego formation.

Over three decades I have probably engaged in hundreds of fantasies with elementary school-age boys, usually seven or eight, about the struggle between good and evil. The struggle between good and evil has taken the form of cops and robbers, Americans against Sadam Hussein, Indians versus cowboys, spacemen versus the aliens or androids. In countless ways, these children expressed their attempt to control the hostile, destructive impulses within them, which they externalized in the various fantasy battles and wars that we would fight in our therapy sessions on the same or opposing sides.

In these battles they reveal their own struggle to determine what is right and what is wrong, and usually they would insist on being the good guy. I have found this kind of play more characteristic of boys than girls, who are more likely to play with my dolls and create fantasies that more directly reveal their family dynamics and peer relations.

Latency-age children make up a large proportion of the cases that are referred and treated. I do not think that it is because preschoolers have fewer problems. Parent-child relationships during the earliest years are very close and exclusive, and often the idea of having to seek help stirs up a great deal of guilt and narcissistic injury in parents. What goes on in the family setting is largely hidden from the scrutiny of outsiders. However, the latency child by contrast is less close to the parents. When he goes to elementary school, he is exposed to the expectations of outside authorities. Latency children are often referred by school personnel. When these children are evaluated, it is not unusual to learn their disturbances were rooted in conditions overlooked during the preschool years.

Some presenting difficulties are especially characteristic of the latency child—like learning problems, problematic peer relations, school phobias, and homesickness. But these problems are not necessarily caused by current conflicts.

I treated a nine-year-old girl I will call Janie, who had developed a school phobia so severe that she had to be carried kicking and screaming to school, pleading with her parents not to leave her. Shortly afterward the school authorities would notify her parents that she was ill in the nurse's office and had to be taken home. She was obsessed with the idea that her friends and her teachers disliked her and preferred others. Treatment revealed that her school phobia related to her murderous fantasies involving her parents, and she had to stay home from school lest they come true. The parents admitted that they had beaten Janie when she was two and a half, because she had developed a sleep disturbance and would scream and cry. Janie's case will be discussed more fully in chapter 8.

In this case the parents had been abusive, but it is not unusual for early latency children to complain teachers and mothers are very mean to them, when in actuality they are not. As one comes to know these children, it becomes clear that they attribute the harsh voice of conscience to outside authorities. The newly formed superego is hard to integrate because it is usually quite severe and uncompromising. Children have to learn that one does not have to be perfect and that there are big, medium, and little crimes. How often I have pointed out to such children that because they may have wished a sibling or parent dead does not mean they actually would kill them. It just means that they sometimes get very angry with the person they also love.

Clearly, emotionally troubled latency-age children are not likely to fit Freud's description of the latency-age child's personality characteristics. A severe form of maladjustment often comes about when the child's fantasies are not merely thought and felt but acted out. Children with passive feminine or masochistic fantasies often succeed in getting bullied and attacked. Sadistic fantasies tend to be acted out by torturing the helpless or by watching others mistreat somebody; I will now describe such a case.

I began treatment with a six-year-old boy I will call Miles, who was probably one of the most maliciously sadistic children I have seen in treatment. It was his teacher who complained about the child's aggressiveness and his tendency to disrupt her class. The mother preferred to see her son as just an energetic kid with strong emotions. It was when the school was considering expelling him that she sought treatment for him. The teacher reported that he had seriously injured other children. He kicked them in the genitals, terrorized them by squeezing their testicles, and punched them in the stomach. Clearly he did not fit the profile of the typical latency child. His mother, however, did not accept the teacher's description of her child or her diagnosis of his problem. The only problems she could identify in my first interview with her were his need to be near her all the time when they are at home and his pattern of waking up in the middle of the night and coming into the parent's bedroom. Only with questioning about his toilet training did she reveal that he soiled, but hastened to tell me that this had only occurred in the last couple months. In subsequent sessions I learned his encopresis had started much earlier, beginning with withholding his bowels. This symptom was minimized in importance by the mother by claiming that he just got caught up playing and did not want to stop to go to the bathroom. The father also excused the child's behavior. He said that one needs to be tough in this world to get what you want. "Miles is like me," he said. "If he wants something, he is relentless in going after it. I'm like that too." He spoke with pride. But he did not like how Miles would shout at them, telling them they were bad parents and then proceed to have a tantrum.

At five weeks of age, Miles was diagnosed with tetralogy of Fallout, and surgery was advised to repair it when he was twelve to eighteen months of age. The surgery to close his heart was performed when he was one and a half, and it left a deep scar center just below his neck.

As I mentioned before, Miles was a very hostile, sadistic child. It was about two months into treatment when Miles began to act out his aggression and his destructive tendencies in his sessions with me. He increasingly displayed his sadistic pleasure in his attempts to injure me, my plants, my property. Once he picked up a good-sized chair and threatened to hit me with it. At this point I vacated my interpretative stance and told him if he did not set the chair down instantly, he had to leave. He set it down. His mother reported this incident while she was driving: Miles brutally pummeled her with his fists, when she refused to take him to a playground because he kept using foul language. In another therapy session he started to throw objects at my glass windows and, this time, he ignored my limit setting. Instead he tried almost successfully to push me out of the office proper, until I warned him if he did not stop I would call the police. He stopped instantly. Like with his mother, he could easily ignore my limits on his aggressive behavior; the police represented a powerful, frightening authority. His father had great difficulty in containing his rage and had been verbally and physically abusive toward this child and his mother. Miles abused his mother the way his father abused the two of them, and now he developed a mother transference to me.

Another theme in the initial stages of treatment was his marked separation anxiety, manifested in his constantly having to check on his mother for fear she might leave him, as well as his having to shadow her at home. He seemed relieved when I told him that children often have murderous thoughts about their parents; but the thoughts do not kill the parents, and parents do not leave the children because they have such thoughts. These interpretations opened the door for him to express these murderous fantasies in his therapy.

At the end of the first year of treatment the mother reported he was doing much better. His anal talk and play had subsided. The parents used his progress as a reason why they could take a long-delayed two week vacation abroad without him. When they returned, they found that massive regression had occurred. Miles was enraged that the father had spirited his mother away and left him behind. The night when they came home, they found several notes in various places in the house with such words as shit, motherfucker, fuck. They also discovered he had urinated on the rug in one of their rooms.

Shortly after this experience, Miles played out this fantasy in his therapy session: I was assigned to be a five-year-old; he told me he would be eight. We both were supposed to have a knife, but his was much bigger and made of silver; mine was made of rubber and much inferior. I was to envy his knife and to wish I could have it. I was to try to steal it from him while he was asleep. One can perceive reversal at play, as in the identification with the fantasized father figure. I was assigned the role of the impotent child.

In one of the last sessions this fantasy was played out, he was patronizing and placating, trying to make me feel OK about having this inferior phallic symbol. Suddenly he threatened to kill me with his knife. I asked in a bewildered tone why he wanted to do this. He became confused as he tried to explain it to me. He said his father's brother killed their father, his grandfather. I asked: Could it be that sometimes boys get angry with their fathers because they spend too much time with their mothers? "That's it!" he exclaimed. Then, as if this idea were too disturbing to him he firmly stated: "I don't want to play this anymore." Then, he told me, "Shut up," accompanied by some of his four-letter words.

About two years after treatment began (Miles was now eight), he was able to tell me about how self-conscious he was about his 2½-inch scar just below his neckline, left by his heart surgery at eighteen months. He feared children would tease and humiliate him, if they saw it. This admission introduced the following fantasy:

He grabbed a letter opener and threatened to cut off my penis. As usual he assigned me the role of a man. Then he turned the knife on himself and made out as if he were cutting off his genitals. "I'm cutting off my penis. Hypnotize me and make me cut off my penis." I thought his concern and anxiety about his surgical scar heightened his castration anxiety. I told him that I had to understand what was going on before I could play in this story. He explained that I was a big guy whom he attacks. He told me that I was the richest guy in the world, and he wanted to cut off my penis. I responded: "I understand now. You want to kill me and take all my riches, everything, maybe my wife, because you're afraid I want to do that to you." Miles aimed the letter opener at his penis, pretending to cut it off.

He resumed this play in a subsequent session. He held a dagger-like letter opener and pretended to stab himself in his genitals. I asked if he were punishing himself by doing what he thought the doctors had done to him. But he responded: "I want your big penis. I want to put it on my penis; I want to cut off my penis and put on your big penis. I was going to kill you." "I get it," I said. "Because you want to kill me to have my big penis, you think I'm angry and want to cut off your penis. Well, I just want you to grow up so you will have a big penis too."

Miles next introduced some blatantly sexual themes into his sessions. Just prior to these fantasies I noted that when leaving the session, Miles frequently attempted to spy on his mother in the reception room by barely opening the door, hoping to peek at her without her being aware of it. I simply commented that he seemed to want to catch his mother doing something he thought she did not want him to see.

He told me that he wanted to change the story now. He giggled and shot embarrassed glances at me. He selected a male and female doll and ordered me to put them in the bedroom. I asked what I was supposed to do with them. He spelled out sex. Miles proceeded to introduce blatantly sexual themes into his sessions. As he set up the scene for his sexual fantasies, he giggled and shot embarrassed glances at me. He used a male and female doll in his fantasy. He ordered me to put them in the bedroom. I asked what I was supposed to do with them. Looking very uncomfortable, he at first said he was not going to tell me, but finally he spelled out the word sex. He took over. He placed the male on top of the female and moved them in a coital rhythm. He had a boy doll put a video camera through a peep hole in order to watch. He said the girl doll was the boy doll's sister. (Miles was an only child.) Next he had the sister discover that her brother was spying. She became enraged with him. He tells her it is wrong for her to have sex when she is not married, and Mom and Dad would not approve of what she was doing, because she is not married. Miles added that his parents only had sex to have him. Here you see his conflict over his masturbatory, voyeuristic fantasies and the common belief that latency children want to hold—namely, that their parents are celibate.

Two and a half years after treatment began Miles was able to tell me about how self conscious he was about his 2½-inch scar just below his neckline, left by heart surgery he had at eighteen months. He feared children would tease and humiliate him, if they saw it. This admission introduced the following fantasy: he grabbed a letter opener and threatened to cut off my penis. As usual he assigned me the role of a man. Then he turned the knife on himself and made out as if he were cutting off his penis.. "I'm cutting off my penis. Hypnotize me and made me cut off my penis.: I told him I had to understand what was going on before I could play in this story with him. He explained that I was a big guy whom he attacks. He told me I'm the richest guy in the world, and I want to cut off his penis. I responded: "I understand now. You want to kill me and take all my riches, everything that I have, maybe even my wife." Miles aims the letter opener at his penis, pretending to cut it off.

In a subsequent session he began the fantasy he wanted to play out with me by grabbing the dagger like letter opener and pretended to stab himself in the genitals. "I'm cutting off my penis. Hypnotize me and make me cut off my penis." I asked if he were punishing himself by doing what he thought the doctors had done to him. He responded: "I want your big penis. I want to put it on my penis; I cut off my penis and put it on your big penis. I was going to kill you." "I get it," I said. "You're jealous of my big penis and you want it. You think I'm angry with you? Well, I just want you to grow up so you will have a big penis too."

Miles next introduced some blatantly sexual themes into his sessions. Just prior to to these fantasies I noted that again Miles attempted to spy on his mother in the reception room by barely opening the door. I suspected it had something to do with his plan to play out some sexual fantasies, for I noticed he lowered his voice. I simply commented that I wondered if he was worried his mother could hear him.

He told me that he wanted to change the story now, and as he did, he giggled and shot embarrassed glances at me. He used a male and female doll in his fantasy. He ordered me to put them in the bedroom. I asked what I was supposed to do with them. Looking very uncomfortable, he at first said he was not going to tell me but finally spelled out sex. He took over; he placed the male on top of the female and into the air moved them in a coital rhythm. He had a teen aged brother of the girl gain access to a video camera and a peep hole in his sister's bedroom so he could watch them. "Have them do it," Miles told me; but he took over and showed me what he said was the correct way. When I commented that he seemed to know a lot about it, he responded: "No, I don't. I haven't seen it. Yeah, I saw it on TV." Next he had the sister discover that her brother was spying; she became enraged with him. He was shocked and then he informed me that their parents don't have sex, only when they had the two of them. I thought this reflected Miles' wishful thinking regarding his own parents.

In the last year of treatment a disturbing incident occurred. Miles's mother telephoned me to relate that Miles had shot a Nerf gun at his father, hitting him near his eye. She reported that the father became so enraged that he grabbed Miles, threw him to the ground, and began pummeling him with his fists on his buttocks. His rage intensified. He pulled off Miles's pants, took off his own belt, and ferociously beat Miles with it. The mother tried to pull him off, but he pushed her away. I saw the mother on the day she called and informed her this was a reportable offense. Crying hysterically she pleaded with me not to report it. She was terrified of her husband's reaction. She was certain that he would take Miles out of treatment. It was decided that I would meet with the father, warn him of the state law protecting children against physical abuse, the possible consequences of his behavior as it affected Miles, and that this must not happen again.

I began the meeting with the father by inquiring about the injury to his eye. He was clearly touched and relieved that I began the session this way. He spent considerable time telling me how concerned he was about any damage to his eyes, and how upset he was when Miles shot a Nerf ball near his eye. It enraged him, and he only wanted to punish Miles for endangering him in this way. Then he told me he lost it; he could not stop himself from beating his son unmercifully. He only stopped when his wife tugged at him to stop. I said that I imagined that it might have been so disturbing to him that he lost control of himself. He then confided that he felt very bad about what he had done. At this point I told him it must not happen again and why. Not only was it brutal treatment of his child, but his child's primary problem involved physically destructive behavior towards others, not an uncommon result of having been treated that way by a parent. I suggested he might consider going into therapy. He said emphatically that it would not happen again. I then informed him about the state laws that govern the physical abuse of children. Not surprisingly, he became angry that the state had the audacity to interfere with the way in which parents discipline their children. He assured me, however, that he would not beat his child again. I instructed both parents to tell Miles that what the father did was wrong, out of order, not the appropriate way to react to what Miles had done to his father, not that Miles's behavior was acceptable. I learned from the mother that when she did convey that to Miles, he burst into tears and said that he so wanted to hear that from her.

For a few weeks after this incident, Miles behaved in his sessions with me in a psychotic-like manner. He would repeatedly fling himself as hard as he could on the floor, attempting to hurt himself, singing in a loud voice, drowning out anything I might say. I suggested that maybe it helped him not to feel so bad about what his dad did to him. He told me to shut up. Finally, after about a two-week period, he took in my interpretations, especially when I said how helpless he must have felt when even his mother could not stop the father. He said in a soft voice: "She did try to stop him. He hit her too."

One day Miles came into his session in a clearly saddened mood. He told me that he was upset that his parents fought terribly and that his father said terrible things to his mother. Miles told her to walk away from his father, but she didn't. She kept fighting with him. His father said to his mother: "You've got your head so far up your butt that you can't think." He then went on to recount in great detail the time his father beat him with his belt after first ripping off his pants. He ended the session by saying that he wished that there could be a family meeting to get his father to stop behaving the way he does. When he took this up with his mother, she said it would be useless, because his father wouldn't listen. I asked if he wanted us to have a meeting with his father at my office. He was so pleased with that idea; but when I asked if he could explain what was upsetting him to his father, he said he wanted me to speak first and then he would talk.

At this meeting the parents entered the room looking quite cowed. I asked Miles if he would like to begin by telling him why we wanted this meeting. He said he wanted me to start. I said that Miles has been quite upset by the fighting that goes on between the two of them. He is upset by the loud screaming and the terrible language that you have used. He is having trouble in school because he is using the same terrible language, and he feels you are setting a very bad example for him. I turned to Miles and asked if I was accurate in saying what I did. He nodded that I was. I went on to add that Miles is working very hard with me, working on understanding his angry outbursts and ways to control them. He has created stories in which he tries to design the foolproof way to avoid explosions and exercise control over them. You are a model for him. The parents were surprisingly meek and quiet. At this point Miles said in a very soft voice: "You may think that what Esther is saying is stupid, but I don't." The father also responded equally softly. "Why would I think it was stupid? I don't." Miles was clearly very pleased. Soon after this exchange Miles asked his parents to leave because he did not want this meeting to take away any more of his time with me. After they left, he raised his hand to slap mine in victory. Then Miles became engaged in a fantasy in which he and his brother completed the design of an airplane that will not be revealed until the year 2035. Despite many harrowing experiences, the newly designed plane survived.

When the treatment was terminated, Miles had received a glowing report card from his school. He had a good summer camp experience, and his mother reported that his relationship with his father had decidedly improved.

This is a case that is an example of how some latency-age children do not fit the profile of the typical latency child. Troubled children like Miles often do not; however, I do believe that when he completed his psychotherapeutic experience, he came much closer to fitting the profile. This case is also an example of the need to work with parents as well as the child.

Rona Knight (2005) did a comprehensive study of latency-age children; four boys and six girls. She followed them from age six to age eleven. They were tested with the Rorschach and the TAT (Thematic Apprehension Test). In addition they were given the Wechsler Bellevue Intelligence Test. Care was taken in only selecting fairly well-adjusted children for the study. There was special interest in examining attachments and autonomy. Both genders exhibited oppositional behavior at home, but in the projective, girls turned anger against themselves, whereas boys directed outward. In this study both parents and children were interviewed. One interesting finding was that early-latency boys experienced their mother as dead to them, and the girls experienced the father as dead—apparently their way of resolving their oedipal attachment and enabling autonomous functioning. Knight points out the multiple tasks the latency child must confront in this period that involves psychosexual development, object relations, separation, and ego and superego development.

Martin Silverman's paper on latency is excellent. It clearly articulates the classical point of view. His article primarily focuses on girls' development in latency; but it does provide some contrast with boys' development as well, and I will review those comparisons.

First of all, Silverman claims that girls have less urgency to relinquish or repress oedipal interests. He suggests that in part this may be due to more societal opposition to boy's incestuous feelings toward their mothers.

The Oedipus conflict, he writes, is more complicated in girls, because of their wish to get something from the father—a baby, penis, and a narcissistic feeding.

Silverman also maintains that girls have more ego controls. Especially in the five to eight years range, girls tend to be precocious and more capable than boys; whereas boys tend to be more fidgety and they have a greater need to suppress their oedipal, sexual feelings due to castration fears.

The nature of their problems differs. Boys tend to have more behavioral and leaning problems, and girls suffer more from depression, low self-esteem, withdrawal, and narcissistic injury.

The content of their fantasies is different. It is not uncommon for girls to have masochistic fantasies—robbers who want to kill them with a knife. Silverman interprets this fantasy as expressing the underlying wish to be penetrated by the father, fused with the guilt wish to be punished by mother for wanting to kill her and possess the father. Boys are more into using phallic symbols, knives, guns, paler forms of Miles's fantasies expressing castration fears. Boys often pretend to be sports heroes or imagine that they can be successfully competitive against celebrity sport figures—father surrogates. When Miles's fantasies became less sadistic, less disturbed, he had such a fantasy—a healthier form of his oedipal rivalry.

The triangular rivalry, the need for a best friend which excludes a third person, is more characteristic of girls than boys. It appears to be a derivative of the Oedipal conflict, where the yearning for the father is transformed into a homosexual longing.

Silverman attributes much more maturity to the female. He reports that girls are less impulsive, learn more quickly, and are less aggressive than boys. The female superego operates with less harshness. He described the latency male superego as more rigid and unyielding. Silverman attributes some of these differences in behavior to varying cultural expectations, depending on the child's sexual identity.

Solnit and Call also provide a well-written presentation of the latency period from the Freudian view. They divide the stage into early and late latency. Like Silverman they describe the overly harsh, punitive superego of the early-latency phase—how guilt feelings are usually managed by projection—the tendency to blame others for things the child has actually done. They point out that in late latency the child tends to be more integrated with his peer group and moves away from the incestuous attachments.

He is now more capable of controlling drive tension, able to postpone drive tension, and thereby more likely to engage in thought as trial action.

I thought it interesting that Solnit and Call claim that late latency is a time when children are likely to become disillusioned with their parents, and these authors describe this as desirable. Parents are no longer viewed as omnipotent, as powerful and godlike. I have often counseled parents who have been troubled by lies their children tell them, that in some ways their lying is a kind of developmental milestone. They have come to realize that their thoughts are private—that parents are not omniscient; they cannot read their minds. I liked one of the last statements in the paper: "While the term *latency* may suggest a period of quiescence, what seems to be taking place is a quiet revolutionary change in the organization of all aspects of mental life."

The next chapter provides another example of a child treated with psychoanalytically oriented psychotherapy.

Chapter Five

Guidelines for a Positive Therapeutic Outcome

There is an increasing popularity of behavioral therapies for the treatment of children as well as adults. This inspired me to review the classical psychoanalytic guidelines for a positive therapeutic outcome—an approach that provides the patient with self-knowledge, an understanding of how his/her mind works, and why. This paper will be divided into three parts: 1) a review of the guidelines of a favorable outcome of psychoanalytic-based therapy; 2) a detailed case presentation of a six-year-old boy in psychoanalytically oriented psychotherapy; and 3) a discussion of some psychoanalytic-based interpretations in the boy's sessions and their effect in the treatment outcome.

To grasp psychoanalytic goals in treatment, it helps to understand development in terms of its psychosexual stages and characteristic defenses, and also to understand the emergence of defense mechanisms in terms of ego development. For example, before a child can use repression as defense, he has to achieve a distinction between ego and id. Projection and introjection require a certain differentiation of the self from the environment, making the understanding of the patient's earliest object relations crucial in analytic treatment. It is hypothesized that child development follows a sequence of libidinal stages, oral, anal, phallic, and oedipal, then latency, puberty, and adolescence, followed by a mature genital phase. The concepts of regression and fixation are essential ones as well.

Object constancy is a central concept in classical developmental theory; it refers to the capacity to distinguish between objects and to maintain a relationship to one specific object, regardless of whether his needs are satisfied. If a child achieves object constancy, he can maintain a positive, internalized image of his mother, whether or not she is present. This is crucial for individuation and separation from the mother. It continues to be essential for all important relationships in one's life and therefore important to examine in analytic treatment.

Anna Freud recognized the importance of the earliest object relationships in the formation of early structure. It was realized that when there is an inadequate resolution of the dyadic stage issues, there will be interference with the resolution of the oedipal problems. It was also recognized that the most severe pathology stems from the early failure in the pre-oedipal period. Many proponents of the developmental point of view believed that the analyst might supply the patient with what was missing in his development: it was postulated that psychoanalysis might revive and repeat the original developmental process now in a way that could be helpful by representing an ideal parental figure for the child. However, there were those who claimed that such an approach tended to sidestep the importance of underlying archaic conflicts, defense and ego states; it would introduce into the therapeutic process parameters that would violate the rule of neutrality on the part of the analyst. From the classical viewpoint, it is usually the changes in superego attitude that are considered the outcome of a corrective emotional experience.

It was Freud who wrote: "The new superego now has the opportunity for a sort of alter-education of the neurotic. It can correct mistakes for which his parents were responsible in educating him," suggesting that the corrective emotional experience progresses from an identification with the analyst. Freud was aware of the importance of the educative function treatment. He wrote: "We cannot avoid taking some patients for treatment who are so helpless and incapable of ordinary life that for them one has to combine analytic with educative influence, and even with the majority, occasions now and then arise in which the physician is bound to take up the position of teacher and mentor" (p. 243). Surely this quote suggests that Freud had a corrective emotional experience in mind for certain categories of patients. According to this view, the purpose of classical psychoanalysis is change via interpretations of unconscious conflicts by pointing out its manifestations in three areas; the past, the present, and the transference.

Harold Blum views the corrective experience as an effort on the part of the analyst to gratify or supply the patient with what was missing in his own development, and he claims that such an approach tends to sidestep the importance of analyzing archaic conflicts, defenses, and ego states. Nevertheless, he wonders whether the psychoanalytic situation itself is a "holding" facilitating environment which, given the analyst's special qualities of empathy and acceptance, would remobilize developmental tendencies within the patient without the necessity of interpreting conflict. Blum concludes, however, that while important, the nurturing aspects of the analytic process are not a substitute for understanding and interpretation, which also encompass an analysis of defenses. With regard to the interpretation, which also encompasses an analysis of defenses, it is important to sound a cautionary note: some defenses are adaptive and should not be disturbed by analytic intervention.

I would like to examine the relationship between the corrective emotional experience and the therapeutic alliance from the classical point of view. The likelihood is that those who have elaborated upon this concept, namely Zetzel and Greenson, would object to equating the therapeutic alliance with the corrective emotional experience. Zetzel's concept involved the idea that there is an alliance between the analyst and the reasonable part of the patient's ego, that a distinction could be drawn between the therapeutic alliance and transference. She maintained that the analyst must be like a good mother with intuitive adaptive responses, that the therapeutic alliance was a recapturing of a very early relationship between mother and infant in which the infant turned to the mother for help in a way that the patient now turned to the analyst. Greenson actually used the term "working alliance." He stressed that "Essentially the humanness of the analyst is expressed in his compassion, concern, and therapeutic intent toward the patient."

James Strachey (1969) described the analytic view of the function of the neurotic symptom. He stated that it was "to defend the patient's personality against an unconscious trend of thought that was unacceptable to it, while at the same time gratifying the trend up to a certain point. It seems to follow, therefore, that if the analyst were to investigate and discover the unconscious trend and make the patient aware of it—if he were to make what was unconscious conscious—the whole raison d'être of the symptom would cease and it must automatically disappear." However, when it did not, Strachey concluded that the task "is not so much to investigate the objectionable unconscious trend as to get rid of the patient's resistance to it" (p. 275). "The fact that the mutative interpretation is the ultimate operative factor in the therapeutic action of psychoanalysis does not simply imply the exclusion of many other procedures (such as suggestion, reassurance, abreaction, etc.) as elements in the treatment of any particular patient" (p. 290).

After Anna Freud published *Ego and the Mechanisms of Defense* in 1936, classical psychoanalysts focused on "ego analysis" rather than "id analysis." The unconscious was no longer interpreted directly in a "classical analysis"; it was to be approached through an analysis of the defenses. Furthermore, Anna Freud and others demonstrated that the hierarchal patterning of defenses varied with the structure of the ego and the nature of the neurosis, so that an obsessive compulsive was described as using characteristic defenses such as isolation, reaction formation, and undoing—a hysteric used other: repression, denial conversion, and phobia. Eissler (1953) proposed that analytic technique should and does vary with the structure of the ego, and in accordance with the hierarchal arrangement of the defense mechanisms.

It is obvious that there are important differences between an adult analysis and the treatment of a child. A young child's anxieties are usually expressed in his or her fantasies that are played out in the therapy sessions, using toys or art materials. The therapist often role-plays in these fantasies and presents interpretations in that role. The adult sits in a chair or lies on a couch. The following example is a description of a play session with a young child.

A four-and-a-half-year-old girl I will name Sue was referred to me because she had suffered from a severe school phobia since she was three years old. The parents had to carry her out, screaming, from nursery school. As she was about to start kindergarten, her parents felt they should seek help for her. Her history was a fairly normal one, although when she was two, her pediatrician discovered she had a heart murmur. She was put under the care of a pediatric cardiologist. I will describe a session that took place just before school started. This was one month after therapy began. She began the session by saying she wanted to talk to me about something that was worrying her. She was going to school on Monday, and she was afraid. I said that we would try to find out what frightened her about going to school. We could pretend it was the first day of school. As we approached the imaginary school, she pretended she was very frightened, hiding behind me, even shaking. I encouraged her to meet her new teacher and she cautiously offered her hand to the imaginary teacher. Suddenly she behaved like a baby. Her speech became infantile, and she could hardly walk. I said that she seemed to feel like a little baby who cannot take care of herself. I knew that she really wasn't a baby—a baby could not dance and sing and learn to read as she was beginning to do.

Suddenly she pretended to be ill. She lay down on the couch, and she told me she was having a heart attack. She instructed me in my role as teacher to sit down, close my eyes, and do nothing. I said that I thought I understood one of the reasons she was afraid of going to school. She was afraid she would become sick, her mother would not be there to take care of her, and her teacher would not have the eyes to see that she was ill. I assured her that this was not so. The school phobia disappeared after this session. Of course, this was just the beginning of our work together. She had many other fears to understand and work out. However, she was able to go to school.

Another important difference between adult and child treatment is that it is crucial for the therapist to have ongoing contact with parents in order to develop a therapeutic alliance with them and to help them understand their child better and in order for the therapist to have a better grasp of the child's reality.

Case Study

Jason, six years of age, was referred for treatment because he was extremely disruptive, hyperactive, and uncooperative in school. He fought with the other children, and he sassed his teachers; finally he was placed in a special class for disruptive children. He also showed signs of a serious learning difficulty. His parents were divorced, and Jason was living with his mother at the time of referral; however, during his first couple of years, the father was the primary caretaker, as the mother worked, and he was a neglectful caretaker. At thirteen months Jason fell down some stairs and suffered multiple fractures of the skull, because the father had failed to watch him carefully. The father had excessively high expectations for Jason; he was rarely satisfied with his developmental progress. The father began to beat Jason when the child was fifteen months of age. The beatings primarily were related to Jason's resistance to toilet training. Jason continued to be enuretic until the time it was understood in therapy.

I saw Jason in psychotherapy twice weekly for almost three years. I also saw his mother in counseling sessions every other week; in addition, she was in individual therapy with someone else. During this period the mother moved from a very hostile, rejecting attitude toward her child to one in which she came to view him with great pride and pleasure.

Jason and his mother came to California from New York when Jason was five. At that time the mother had just left Jason's father and was now living with a new boyfriend. In short order the father appeared in the scene. He began to see Jason on a regular basis while the mother filed for divorce. Jason seemed to care a great deal about his father. He expressed a wish that his parents get back together again; Jason also told me that the father called him names: "jerk," "stupid," and "son of a bitch."

The father was a movie buff and very often took Jason to movies or watched films on late-night TV with him; however, many of them were rated R; and even possible X-rated ones, filled with violence" and explicit sexual scenes. Although the father was apparently a bright man, he led a rather marginal life; he chose to work as little as possible, occasionally making minimum wages at menial work. The mother, however, made a fairly good income as a nurse.

Jason described his father as a house husband, and indeed until the parents separated, the father stayed home and took care of the child. He had wanted his wife to abort this child, but she very much wanted him and went ahead with the pregnancy despite her husband's disapproval. The mother claimed that the father did not want to take on the responsibilities involved, and in addition was very jealous of Jason; he claimed that she paid too much attention to Jason and not enough to him.

The mother breast-fed Jason for the first seven months, at which time she claimed he weaned himself. She was working full-time and pumped her breasts so someone else could feed him. He had early feeding problems. He had difficulty in shifting from pureed food to solid food, which would infuriate the father, who would insist that he eat.

The mother reported that Jason was toilet trained at thirteen months and claimed that it was because he wanted to imitate his father. Later she admitted that both she and the father were extremely impatient with Jason and wanted him trained at this early age; however, Jason continued to wet his bed almost up until the last months of therapy, when it was finally resolved in treatment. When Jason was fifteen months of age, the father began to spank him. The father seemed to have very high expectations for his child, who always seemed to disappoint him in whatever effort he was making.

When Jason was three and a half years of age, the parents went on vacation and left him with his grandmother. While he was there he developed otitis media, and the grandmother had him hospitalized. The parents did not return at this time, and the child reacted intensely to their absence. The mother believed that Jason's personality changed dramatically after the hospitalization. Whereas he had been very cooperative prior to the hospitalization, he now became stubborn and oppositional. There were complaints at his preschool that he was a problem child.

Treatment

From the outset, Jason seemed to feel very positive about "counseling," as he called the therapeutic process. Throughout the treatment, Jason used the metaphor of play to explore and to understand his conflicts and express his feelings of deprivation. His fantasies seemed to provide the proper distance that made it possible for him to examine his problems. Nevertheless, there were those times when Jason would discuss his feelings regarding the separation and divorce of his parents, or his feelings about school, friends, his teachers, his enuresis, his resentment toward his mother and her new boyfriend and his anger toward his father, but more likely his conflicts and feelings of parental neglect or inadequacy would be expressed in fantasy.

I found Jason to be a very bright, attractive-looking, imaginative six-year-old, with a certain appealing cocky attitude that sometimes became a petulant and disgruntled one. In the early phases of therapy, I too observed his short attention span. He would flit from one thing to another, abruptly interrupting one activity to go on to another. Usually his fantasies included some conflict between good and evil. I was usually relegated to playing the bad guy, whom he would overpower. Some of the themes focused on his resentment toward a neglectful mother figure. He delighted in playing parents who rejected their children, and who had contempt for their children's neediness. He very often depicted parents having sexual intercourse. He reveled in showing how knowledgeable he was about sexuality, at the same time revealing his confusion about it.

In the initial stage of the therapy, Jason was very open and eager to let me know how much he liked coming to see me. As the therapy proceeded and he became more involved with me, he developed a coolness and toughness, an "I don't care" attitude. It was a thin cover for how much the therapy meant to him; for, if he missed a few minutes at the beginning of a session, he became irritable and demanded that it be made up at the end of the session. The struggle between good and evil took the form of cops and robbers, Nazis against Americans, Indians versus cowboys and spacemen versus the aliens or the anthropoids, Sitting Bull versus Wild Bill Hickok, Mexicans versus Texans, Americans versus the Japanese or Russians. In countless ways, I felt that Jason expressed his attempt to control his hostile, destructive impulses, which he externalized in the various fantasized battles and wars that we fought on the same or opposing sides. Those battles became the most persistent fantasy that he introduced into the therapy, and they continued up until the very last session.

Another recurrent theme in the therapy was maternal neglect. In the fourth month of therapy, he had the following fantasy about a family of two sons and one daughter. The parents, apparently in an attempt to get away from the children, decided to sleep in the meadow. When I inquired as to what they were doing there, Jason told me: "They were probably humping." The children had been left in the forest and, during the night, they were attacked by a robber. The daughter found the parents and reported to them that the son was unconscious. The mother responded, "It's nothing. I'm a nurse." In actuality, Jason's mother tended to minimize illnesses and very often would send Jason to school when he complained of feeling ill.

There were many sequences in which Jason used the Ken and Barbie dolls for his fantasy play. Sometimes he would cover them with Kleenex so they could have privacy, Jason explained. During this phase, he was rather seductive with me, and he would attempt to exhibit himself. One time he was in the bathroom and called to me to join him. I told him that here, people have privacy in the bathroom. "Esther, I have something very interesting to tell you," he said. I told him I could hear him from where I was. Once he realized that I was not going to join him in the bathroom, he called out to me: "I'm only six years old and I wear a size ten underwear!" When I rejoined that he was very big for his age, he was very pleased to agree with me. I should have added that it seemed important to him to let me know how big he was.

It was typical for Jason to depreciate me and call me names and to attempt to make me feel stupid and inadequate. Both his parents related to him in this way. Once, while we were playing cavalry (he was the commander in chief and I, the sergeant), he claimed everything I did was inept. I was called stupid at every turn until finally I complained about this abusive behavior. I told him that when I was a little boy (for in the play I was instructed to be a man), my father called me names like stupid and jerk, especially when I did not get things right the first time. I complained that everyone should be able to make mistakes while they are learning something. I added: "When you call me 'dumbbell,' it reminds me of my father. "He looked rather thoughtful and somewhat saddened, and finally he said, "Maybe you should hang around more with your mom." However, on another occasion when there was similar play and similar deprecatory treatment, I complained that he was a perfectionist not allowing anyone to make any mistakes. He countered, "Better to be a perfectionist than dumb."

Jason brought in material related to the traumatic effects of his hospitalization in a most interesting manner. One day he was looking at the books in my office and inquired about "the wolfman." He paged through the book and wanted to know why they called this man "the wolfman." He certainly looked normal enough, he added. I said that it was because he had a dream about wolves, a nightmare. "I have a nightmare," he told me. "They're the only kind of dreams I have. I have had a nightmare for three years, since I was four years of age. My mother's friends are in it; they are good friends who live in New York. I'm with them and my mother; but I get separated from them. The aliens come and take me away. They cover me with oil and put me in a covered pot. They're going to set the pot on fire. Instead it makes me stronger and stronger like Superman. Finally I break out of the pot and I can fly. I fly away from the alien ship." I asked him if this meant that there was a happy ending. "No," he said. "Because I never find my mother again." I inquired if he had ever been separated from his mother, as far as he knew. "I've never left her," he told me. "She always leaves me. She's always going off to work." I wondered if he were sometimes scared that she would not come back. But Jason had spent long enough with this dream and wanted to play out the fantasy of the Mohawk Indians in combat with the cavalry. This fantasy play allowed for an escape from his anxiety and his painful thoughts and fears of abandonment.

In the next session I told him that I had thought a lot about his dream, because it was interesting, and because dreams usually contain a wish. Sometimes they tell us what we are afraid of and how we try to get rid of the fear. He repeated the dream, and this time he told me that when the aliens put him in the heater and he fell into the oil, he exploded, after which he had the strength of a thousand men. This made it possible for him to fly away. I told him that I thought his wish was that he would not feel small and helpless and at the mercy of the aliens, people he did not know; he wished he could be strong as a thousand men and get away from them and back to his mother. I pointed out that he mentioned that his mother left him to go to work, but I wondered if there was a time when he might have been away from his mother in a scary place like a hospital with people he did not know who might have done tests on him. "No!" he protested. "My mother never left me. She is a nurse. If I went to the hospital, she was with me."

Jason's mother told me in our next interview that as soon as she had picked him up after this last session, he asked if he had been hospitalized, and his mother confirmed that he had an ear infection while he was staying with his grandmother, who felt that he should be in the hospital. The mother stressed that she did not know about it or she would have been there.

It was a few weeks before the subject of the dream surfaced again. Jason told me that he had watched a friend of his mother nurse her baby, and that he remembered nursing at his mother's breast. I marveled at such an early memory, and he went on to tell me that he remembered being in diapers too. I told him I knew he had a good memory because of how he remembered his nightmare. He made no comment to my reference to his dream, and instead became frightened of a noise he thought he heard outside my office. He became increasingly fearful, and he felt I could not protect him if something were out there. "I'm stronger than you are," he told me. That evening he called me on the telephone to inquire whether I was all right and, with a sigh of relief, said he feared that the Martians might be coming.

In the next session I thanked him for calling me to see if I was safe. I told him that this had happened once before to another boy, who had also worried about me and called me to find out if I were all right. Jason wanted to know who that boy was. I told him that the boy was older than he was—eight years old. "I'm seven," he said. I told him that this boy was concerned for different reasons. Jason wanted to know what those reasons were. I explained that this boy thought that it was the noises that he had heard that were scary, but really he was scared about what he was talking about. "What was he talking about?" Jason wanted to know. I told him that he was talking about a time when he was alone by himself without his parents. "How long was he by himself? I told him it was a couple of days, because he was in a hospital. "Why wasn't his mother with him?" Jason demanded to know. I told him that the mother had left him with a babysitter and did not tell her where she was going, so the babysitter couldn't call her. He had developed tonsillitis, and the babysitter had to take him to the hospital. "That couldn't happen to me," he said, "because my mother tells the babysitter where she is. That reminds me," he added, "only once my mother wasn't with me in the hospital." I asked him how old he was, and he told me that he was three at the time. I suggested that might be why he had the same nightmare for four years.

I learned from the mother that following this session, Jason asked if he could have his tonsils out. A few sessions later, when he was looking at the shelves in my office, I asked him if I could get some advice from him. I reminded him of the boy who had his tonsils out in the hospital at a time when his mother left him with a babysitter. I explained that I wanted to ask his advice about the fact the boy now wanted to have his appendix out, even though there was nothing wrong with his appendix. "Why would he want to have his appendix out?" I asked. After some reflection he replied, "His mother is going to be with him, isn't she?" "Are you telling me," I asked, "that he would want to make sure his mother came with him this time?" "Yes, that's the $64,000 answer!" he told me.

In a later session Jason chatted at length about different skits on *Saturday Night Live* and which performers he preferred. He told me that he liked the actors better in the old *Saturday Night Live*; he missed them. I commented that a person gets attached to people and misses them when they are no longer around. He agreed, and he began to reminisce about his friends he had left behind in the East; he told me he missed them. He described how his mother had come out to California before him; later he flew on an airplane to be with her. He was only five, he told me. I suggested that it might have been a little scary to come out by himself. At first he denied it, but then acknowledged that he had been scared.

In the fantasy that followed this discussion, he said that we were in a spaceship designed for landing on the Moon. It was a moon mobile, and we were to be those people in the spaceship. He explained that we were equipped with ray guns and bombs because we might meet up with aliens. We had a robot by the name of Snickers. Jason fought the aliens who attacked us time and again. He dropped bombs on them. At one point, however, he said that he had been away from Earth twelve years; he wanted to return, because he had a message from his wife that she was having a baby. I expressed surprise that he had been away for twelve years and she was now having a baby. Without missing a beat, he immediately responded, "That's right, and it only takes nine months to have a baby. That means my wife is having a baby with another man." He decided to blow up Earth, but after he did, he discovered that his wife and her boyfriend had already fled. He had killed the Earth people for nothing.

The play just described continued the following session. We continued to fight the aliens from our spaceship, but in addition we had to catch the mother ship, and he had to murder his mother and her boyfriend for having a baby together. Jason said that he wanted to handle the murder himself, and so he embarked on the mother ship alone. He returned to tell me that the boyfriend was dead; however, he had spared his wife. I asked what happened to the boyfriend. He told me he had poisoned his food, and that he was dead, but nobody knew that he had murdered him. I said that I was really surprised he was able to get along so well with his wife. I knew how furious he was with her for going off with her lover. "What's the matter with you?" he asked. "Don't you know about 'forgive and forget.'" I told him how much I admired his being able to forgive his wife, to see her faults and still care for her. Jason looked very proud of himself.

I wanted to understand how the specifics of this fantasy might be rooted in the realities of Jason's life; however, when I questioned his mother about this period of time, she was reluctant at first to discuss it. Finally, she confessed to me that she had become pregnant by a lover and had had an abortion shortly before coming to California. It was likely that Jason knew about it, as she had confided in Jason's babysitter while he was present. Jason's fantasy seemed to suggest that he was now ready to forgive what he had obviously not forgotten. Following this play sequence, his separation anxiety lessened considerably, as he continued to work through problems related to it.

I mentioned earlier that Jason had not resolved his enuretic problem until the later phases of therapy. Wetting his bed every night had become an embarrassment to him and he wanted to work on the problem. His enuretic problem had multi-determinants. It was related to his underlying hostility and defiance, his exhibitionism, the breakdown of his defenses against his dependency needs, and lastly his concept of sexuality, which clearly related to his repeated witnessing of the primal scene.

In one session, he played out a fantasy in which he was a baby repeatedly beaten by his mother and so he purposely made his mother think he wet his bed. The mother in this story sought counseling from a woman named Esther. During the consultation, speaking for the mother, he told Esther that the baby wet his bed and I, in the role of Esther, informed the mother that the baby did this not only because he was so young but because he was very angry with her. Suddenly, two policemen broke into the room and arrested the mother for child abuse.

A trial followed. It was held in Germany. Now in the role of the father, Jason testified that the mother beat the child and named the number of lashes the child received from her. Acting as the judge, I questioned the father as to why the mother did this, and he responded that the baby wet and shit in his bed. He then made a point of the fact that the child had been wetting for a year and a half, but the mother had been beating him for two years. I, as the judge, drew the obvious conclusion, that the child wet his bed because of the mother's cruelty. American soldiers broke into the courtroom and announced that the mother was wanted for child abuse in the United States, took her back to America, and shot and killed her. This is an interesting fantasy in that the mother is identified as the abuser and the father is portrayed as the child's ally and protector, when in actuality the opposite was the case. Other material suggested that Jason needed to maintain an idealized image of his father. In fact, he tended to identify with his father's punitive, critical attitudes. I thought his rage toward his mother related to the fact that she had left his father, moreover, she often left Jason in the care of others, and was herself involved in a series of successive love affairs.

As we confronted these issues, Jason began to be dry occasionally at night for the first time. He hoped that he would be dry by the time he went to summer camp. I remarked that we would just have to figure out all the psychological reasons why he wet. "Here we go with all that psychological stuff again," he countered. I enlisted his help in understanding another boy who also wet at night and Jason's explanation was as follows: "Probably it was when he found out his mother was having sex and so he started wetting." I asked him if the boy thought he was having sex too by wetting. "Yeah, you got it," he told me. I responded that it was not urine that comes out when a grown man has sex. With great surprise, he said, "It's not?" He seemed genuinely surprised when I described semen to him and told him how it carried the sperm. He said to me, "That is disgusting." Apparently urinating was not. I told him that now that he knew this, perhaps he could be dry at night, and he was. What Jason was able to tell me was that his conception of sex, when he repeatedly witnessed the primal scene, was an infantile understanding of what transpired. He was a child who was not sexually abused but obviously overstimulated sexually; this led to symptom formation: namely, his enuresis. Of course, his enuresis had multideterminants, among them his underlying hostility and defiance, his exhibitionism, his defense against his dependency needs, and last but not least, his concept of sexuality, which clearly related to his repeated witnessing of the primal scene. The fact that Jason stopped wetting his bed after my interpretive work with him lends credence to the belief that interpretation is the primary mutative factor in psychoanalytic treatment.

Discussion

In my work with Jason, I believe I mostly followed the classical analytic model; however I deviated from strict adherence. I was reassuring instead of interpretive when Jason wanted me to be impressed by the size of his underwear. As for his playing out his fantasies of being a demanding, hostile commander, I believe Jason was attempting to merge with an omnipotent, critical, perfectionistic parent in order to maintain his self-esteem. In my interpretation I was not only pointing out Jason's defensive identification with his father and his projections onto me of his feelings of inadequacy, I was speaking for the battered Jason in an attempt to get him to be more tolerant of himself and perhaps to feel some anger toward his parents' intolerance of his imperfections.

The analysis of defenses is a crucial component of any classical analytic process. Jason externalized his hostile bad self, not only by calling black children "niggers," but also in the many battles of good versus evil in the therapy. The identification with the aggressor was apt in his punitive, hostile attitude toward me when he played out being my commander.

An important element of the classical approach in therapy is reconstruction. Reconstruction was used when I interpreted the dream maternal Jason presented. It seemed to help him integrate the memory of his hospitalization and lessen its deleterious effects, especially as it related to his separation anxiety.

I think it is apparent that Jason's pre-oedipal and oedipal issues framed my thinking about this case, and I believe the changes that occurred in this child were related to the opportunity to play out his oedipal anxieties in the therapy: to murder the father and possess his mother. The fantasy clearly reflected a powerful oedipal conflict. I thought that Jason's comment, "Don't you know about forgive and forget?" reflected a mature resolution of his anxieties. There was a definite lessening of his separation anxiety after this session, and this was after two years of therapy in which he either killed off the mother or sentenced her to death in a court decision. I was probably the wished for dyadic, pre-oedipal mother who would spend twelve years exclusively with him and not the actual mother who was dividing her time between career, social life, and parenting.

You probably noted that I was relegated to playing the bad guy in most cases. It was Jason's parents who were impatient with him during his toilet training period, but in the therapy the child played out actively what he experienced passively at the hands of both parents. *He* was the bad child who wet his bed in the play; but he became the good person and the therapist the bad. His severe superego and his poor self-esteem were reflected in his battles between good and evil, those games when I was called stupid and told: "better to be a perfectionist than dumb!" In this way Jason revealed his identification with his father, his identification with the aggressor. Two aspects of the transference were revealed in this session: 1) the pre-oedipal and oedipal father transference and 2) the splitting of objects into good and bad.

The sexualization of the transference was predictable. Not only was he the only son of a mother who obtained a divorce during the child's oedipal phase, but he had a father who took him to R-rated movies instead of standing between the child and the child's oedipal wishes. Moreover, the child witnessed sexual relations on and probably off the screen; and these overstimulations were bound to appear in the transference, as they did when he asked me to join him in the bathroom so he could show me what big underwear he had to wear, or in his fantasies when he had his parents "humping" in the meadow.

While Jason's treatment markedly differed from that of an adult in psychoanalytically oriented psychotherapy, the underlying goals were similar: 1) to learn about his interactions with his earliest object relations and their effect on him. Both parents were unusually harsh with him; 2) to interpret the defenses he used to ward off psychic pain. Repression was effective in blanketing any memory of his early traumas; 3) to expose what interfered with the development of object constancy, which intensified his separation anxiety; 4) to understand both the mother and father transferences, which helped to clarify his underlying conflicts, as well as his identification with his hostile father who liked to share his sexually explicit movies with his son; 5) to analyze his dreams, which in the therapy revealed his underlying Oedipal conflict and an understanding of his separation anxiety; 6) to focus on resolving his presenting problems—as in his hostile, disruptive behavior at home and at school, his learning problems, and his enuresis; and 7) to provide insight, so Jason could "forgive and forget" and not feel he was such a "bad kid." I thought Jason's comment, "Don't you know about forgive and forget?" revealed a generosity of spirit and an advance in psychic development, and that was after two years in therapy in which he killed off the mother figure or sentenced her to death in court.

At the beginning of this chapter I noted that I was motivated to write on the effectiveness of psychoanalytic treatment because of the increasing popularity of behavioral therapy. In a 1993 study by Jonny Palas, it was noted that the "psychodynamic therapists focused on the evocation of affect, bringing problematic feelings into awareness to integrate current difficulties with previous life experiences: The behavioral therapists, on the other hand, attempted to effect change by stressing "intellect and rationality." They focused on the patient's ability to make decisions and dealt mainly with the patient's ability to make decisions in the current situation. Clearly Jason was in need of a psychodynamic form of therapy.

Freud's original thesis was that psychoanalysis was designed to result in an expansion of the patient's conscious knowledge of certain previously unrecognized aspects of his or her unconscious mental life, which in turn would provide an understanding of the different ways the patient devised during childhood to deflect, alter, disguise and also gratify those wishes, as well as blanket out traumatic memories. Jason repressed the memory of his hospitalization because it was such a traumatic experience for him. Psychoanalytically oriented therapy brought to light the traumatizing effects of that experience and helped to resolve the damaging effects.

Because there has been disagreement as to what was the essential core of psychoanalytic treatment, the American Psychoanalytic Association formed a committee to formulate definitions of the psychoanalytic process (Weinshel, 1990; Boesky, 1990).

The committee was titled COPE and it defined the analytic process as follows: 1) transference, 2) resistance, 3) dynamic unconscious, 4) intrapsychic conflicts, 5) defense, 6) infantile sexuality, and 7) insight that causes change and change that leads to insight. According to Boesky, the analytic process is predicated on assumptions of a dynamic unconscious, the oedipal complex, intrapsychic conflict, and psychic determinism. Strachey stated Freud's view of cure "the function of the neurotic symptom is to defend the patient's personality against an unconscious trend of thought that was unacceptable to it." However, even if the analyst succeeded in making the unconscious conscious, he was likely to meet resistance as I did when Jason resisted acknowledging he felt abandoned when his mother was not with him during his hospitalization. Strachey concludes that the analyst's main task is not so much to investigate the objectionable unconscious as "to get rid of the patient's resistance to it" (p. 275). It is also important to note that psychoanalytic therapy includes supportive interventions as well, and this depends on the patient's needs (Leichsenring, 2002).

Shedler (2004) defined psychoanalytic therapy as "based on psychoanalytic concepts and method that involves less frequent meetings. It explores "those aspects of self that are not fully known." This definition characterizes Jason's twice-weekly sessions; however, COPE's list describes his therapeutic experience as well. George Allison (1994) would probably disagree. He maintains that the difference lies in the greater insight that is obtained in psychoanalysis, and that there is more supportive help offered in psychotherapy. In my therapeutic work with Jason, I believe he achieved remarkable insight into his previously unconscious conflicts. Weinshel (1990) stated that the main objective of therapy is increased self-awareness and insight, and I believe Jason achieved those goals. However, Weinshel also concludes that psychoanalysis is a personal endeavor and the manner in which each analyst translates his/her version of psychoanalytic therapy into clinical technique may border on the idiosyncratic.

I realize that this statement may well apply to Jason's therapy as well. I nevertheless conclude that the therapeutic progress in this case followed the psychoanalytic guidelines for a favorable therapeutic outcome.

Chapter Six

From Autism to Oedipus

It has been contended that some of the most difficult children to treat with psychotherapy are those with infantile autism. They cannot communicate very well because they have meager or inadequate language skills. They tend to relate to others as if they were just inanimate objects in this world. They often stare vacantly, as if they do not see. Sometimes they are thought to be deaf, because they behave as if they do not hear. They have been described as children encapsulated in a shell, cut off from the world around them; yet they often display an inordinate interest and adeptness in working with mechanical objects or puzzles. Their behavior has also been described as repetitive and stereotyped.

Autism is a rare and mystifying disorder. While there is a general consensus that it is a constitutional, genetic, or organic-based deficit, research studies that have attempted to establish this fact have produced inconclusive and contradictory results. The diagnosis of infantile autism can only be based on behavioral observations at the present time. Moreover, there are a multitude of treatment approaches that have been applied in these cases, the proponents of each claiming varying degrees of success. In recent years there has been a marked focus on the neurophysiological and behavior modification approaches to the diagnoses and treatment of autism and a devaluing of the psychodynamic and particularly psychoanalytic perspectives. It is the aim of this paper to underscore and reaffirm the invaluable contribution of psychoanalysis to the understanding and amelioration of the autistic condition.

A brief historical perspective is in order. Isolated cases that strongly suggested an autistic component have been described in the literature for centuries, but it was Leo Kanner, a professor at Johns Hopkins School of Medicine in Baltimore, Maryland, who, in 1943, was to describe the specific symptomatology and to term it "early infantile autism" (Kanner, 1943). Kanner was already known as the author of the first American textbook on child psychiatry. The term itself referred to the self-centeredness and self-absorption of autistic children, and their lack of contact with others in their world. Kanner (1943, 1944) stressed that signs of this disorder, specifically the inability to relate to others in the usual expectable manner, were there from the beginning of life. His case histories describe the blank expression of these children, their need for sameness, the tantrums that occur when their rituals are interrupted. Kanner noted their difficulty in absorbing what is said and responding with appropriate and creative sentences. If, indeed, they go beyond single words and unintelligible speech, echolalia is common. To quote Kanner: "Affirmation is indicated by literal repetition of a question. Personal pronouns are repeated just as heard with no change to suit the altered situation . . . consequently (the child) comes to speak of himself always as 'you' and of the person addressed as 'I.' Not only the words but the event intonation is retained" (1943, p. 243).

In more recent years there has been a marked effort to distinguish this disorder from other childhood psychoses like childhood schizophrenia, symbiotic psychosis, mental retardation with autistic features and severe emotional disabilities. The DSM-III-R (APA, 1987) defines autism only by its clinical behavior because there are no objective pathognomonic biomedical markers common to all cases. It is stated that once autistic, always autistic. There are two distinct types of clinical onset: it may be perceived in the first few weeks of life, or the child may display normal development for twelve to twenty-four months and then regress by manifesting the typical autistic features. Studies have shown that the great majority of autistic children will require lifelong sociosupport systems. There appear to be no distinctions in terms of socioeconomic, racial, or cultural factors.

Once Early Infantile Autism took its place as an officially recognized diagnostic category, there was a proliferation of research studies that attempted to determine its etiology and the most efficacious approach to its treatment. Not surprisingly, the predetermined focus on one or another etiological factor often tended to dictate the suggested therapeutic remedy. Clearly, our interest in this paper is in the treatment of autistic children viewed from a psychoanalytically oriented, psychodynamic perspective; indeed, the body of this presentation will be devoted to that perspective. It is important to underscore, however, that this does not mean that we negate the very strong likelihood that Infantile Childhood Autism has a constitutionally based organic and/or genetic predisposition; on the contrary, we adhere to the belief that autistic children come into this world with a preformed vulnerability to this disorder. In fact, before focusing on our psychoanalytic emphasis, we will briefly review some of the current research work carried out by nonanalytic psychologists and psychiatrists.

Studies over the past thirty years have attempted to isolate neurobiochemical and hematologic abnormalities in autistic children. A study by Schain and Freedman (1961) determined that serotonin levels in the blood of children diagnosed as autistic were significantly higher than in control cases. Some studies have confirmed these findings; others have contradicted them. Ritvo, Yuwiler, Geller, Kales, Rashkis, Schicor, Plotkin, Axelrod, and Howard (1971) demonstrated that L-dopa significantly lowered the blood serotonin concentration in a small sample control study of autistic children, without, however, any concomitant effect on their behavior. Another proposed hypothesis suggested that autistic symptomatology was the result of an altered ability to maintain normal brain serotonin levels. Tryptophan loading and amino acid excretion were studied. Again contradictory results were found. Cohen and his associates (Cohen, Johnson, and Caparulo, 1976) determined the blood lead levels in children with autism and compared them with those of their nonautistic siblings; levels in the former were significantly higher. To date, no one has been able to replicate this finding.

Some researchers, like Ritvo, Ornitz, and La Franchi (1968), have examined the autistic child's disturbance in sensorimotor integration. Many autistic children demonstrate a paradoxical set of reactions to sensory stimulation. On the one hand, they are likely to search out tactile stimulation, create loud unpleasant noises, and at the same time become panic-stricken by sudden noises or lights. Shafi (1979) suggests that it appears to be the unexpected sensory stimuli that are disturbing. Based on this finding, it has been recommended that such children be placed in highly structured situations with predetermined materials to be worked on, and preset, designated time limits.

Rutter together with his collaborators Cox, Bartak, Newman, and Sussenwein (Rutter, 1966, 1967, 1968, 1970, 1972, 1973, 1974; Rutter and Sussenwein, 1971: Rutter and Bartak, 1973; Cox, Rutter, Newman, and Bartak, 1975) has done extensive studies to establish his contention that autism is some form of organic brain disorder. The repetitiveness and stereotypy so characteristic of these children is understood as an outcome of this organicity. He and his associates proposed behavioral modification programs, emphasizing language and cognitive development. In fact, most of the researchers who focus primarily on organic etiology, who only perceive these children as having a brain incapable of normally processing information and, for that matter, all incoming stimuli, tend to see the use of behavioral modification techniques as the treatment of choice. Some, like Ritvo and Freeman (1984), have gone so far as to declare how terrible it has been that psychotherapists have "wasted fruitless years of psychotherapy on children that was supposed to cure their autism. Even more discouraging is the fact that many of our colleagues in the U.S. and abroad still cling to those outmoded and disproven notions, refusing to update their knowledge in the face of current research" (p. 299). It is interesting that while many proponents of behavioral modification programs claim that behavior therapy is far more successful in treating autistic children than traditional forms of child therapy (especially any form of psychoanalytically oriented psychotherapy), they do not cite specific studies that substantiate such conclusions; moreover, as we well know, comparative studies of this kind are suspect anyway in terms of the criteria used and the matching of subjects, as well as the many pitfalls involved in drawing conclusions about treatment outcome.

The hypothesis that the primary difficulty of autistic children lies in their inability to process symbols led Colby (1973) to develop a computer-based treatment program. The method consists of providing the child with a computer with the usual keyboard and monitor, and encouraging the autistic child to play with it. The computer program provides pictures, symbols, and the sounds of human voices. Colby claimed that autistic children were successfully treated with this program, so much so that they began to use speech for social communication. A question that comes to our mind is the appropriateness of using a treatment approach that minimizes human contact with children whose central problem involves an inability to relate to other human beings, unless it is only used as a first step in helping them form object relationships.

Investigators who have identified defective social relatedness as the core problem of autistic children have greatly benefited from the advances in infant research and the systematic study of social interactional processes. Drawing heavily from both psychoanalytic and attachment theory, these investigators have focused on early relationships as possibly providing a key to understanding the phenomena of autistic symptomatology. One line of investigation deals with communication of emotions. There is considerable empirical evidence that infants seem to be programmed to use emotions to communicate even before developing others forms of communication. Brazelton (1982) noted that infants avert their gaze to regulate arousal during emotional exchanges, beginning at about six months. As early as three months they can recognize emotional expression. The autistic child deviates from normal infants in these respects, being incapable of recognizing emotions and using them to communicate.

Bemporad, Ratey, and O'Driscoll (1987) proposed an interesting hypothesis to explain the evolvement of autistic affective withdrawal. They suggest that these children are not able to process their caregivers' emotional signals from birth; they have in a sense a kind of "emotional aphasia," which prevents them from developing affective systems of knowledge. Another prolific writer and researcher in infantile autism, R. P. Hobson (1983, 1990), believes that one develops one's concept of the existence of other persons through relationships and that this is effected through "empathic responsiveness." He further suggests that without this empathic involvement, persons are likely to be experienced as objects, as indeed they appear to be in the case of autistic children. Hobson concludes that the autistic child's deficits in symbolic thinking derive from his deficits in the "prewired" process of affective communication.

Given the increasing interest in the very earliest affective communication of the infant, normal and autistic, more detailed and specific aspects have been studied. Walters, Barrett, and Feinstein (1990) provide an excellent review of the studies in joint attention. They define joint attention as "an aspect of preverbal communication addressing the infant's movement from a dyadic (mother and baby, or baby and object) to a triadic (mother, baby, and object) focus of attention." They state that without the capacity for joint attention, "there is no real motivation to develop language" (1990, p. 312). Many studies have documented the finding that autistic children are clearly deficient in their joint attention capacities.

The term *intersubjectivity* was introduced by Trevarthen and Hubley (1978) to denote the infant's first efforts to share his caregiver's view of the world of objects. Stern (1985) later used the same term to describe the infant's attempts to share objects, attention, and affective states with others. It would seem, however, that the concept of joint attention bears a striking similarity to that of intersubjectivity. More important that the specific term used to describe this phenomenon is the means by which autistic children can be helped to overcome these apparently very early preformed deficits in relating to other human beings. On that note we would like now to review some of the psychoanalytic literature that is relevant to our discussion of autism.

In our estimation, Margaret Mahler (1968, 1979) is perhaps the foremost pioneer in the study of childhood autism, as viewed from a psychoanalytic perspective. Other analytic workers have added immensely to the understanding of autistic children as well as demonstrating effective therapeutic techniques in their treatment: namely, Melanie Klein, Frances Tustin, and Donald Meltzer. Frances Tustin (1981, 1991), in particular, has written voluminously and illuminatingly in the past decade about the autistic condition; but, understandably, she has borrowed heavily from Mahler's formulations and treatment approach. Some of Tustin's unique contributions will be discussed later. At this point we will examine Mahler's conceptualizations.

Mahler based her beginning formulations regarding the development of the infant's undifferentiated rudimentary ego on Freud's early observation that the mother's empathic response to her baby's bodily needs is far more crucial for the survival of the human infant than it is for other mammals. This species characteristic necessitates what Mahler terms a "social symbiosis." Mahler expands on Freud's concept of the formation of the body ego by stressing its first step significance in leading to a sense of individual identity. She also draws from Hartmann, Kris, and Lowenstein's (1979) propositions regarding ego development. "The infant's body is both internal and external at the same time. By virtue of this characteristic, it stands out for him from the rest of the world and thereby enables him to work out the distinction between self and non-self. Proprioceptive inner stimuli, as well as contact perceptions, deep pressure sensitivity and thermal interchange, in addition to kinesthetic experiences . . . in the nursing situation contribute much more importantly and immediately to the core of our feeling of identity, to our body image, than the later maturing distance-perceptive visual and auditory images. The latter contribute primarily and most importantly to the recognition of and distinction from the object world" (Mahler, 1979, p. 173).

Mahler's primary tenet is that "growing up" (i.e., separation and individuation) involves a slow weaning from the mother-infant duality or symbiosis, and object relationships develop both as a consequence of and the differentiation from this symbiosis.

Mahler identified two types of infantile psychoses: autism and symbiosis. In infantile autism she proposed that the child is unable to experience his mother as a need-satisfying object; he, in fact, is incapable of being aware of his own self as distinct from the inanimate environment. Mahler describes the self-destructive activities of these children—the head-knocking, self-biting—as restitutive measure: "To sharpen the awareness of the body-self boundaries, often at the expense . . . of parts of the body image . . . these children are completely impervious to their mother's voice and commands, nor do they seem to see you; they look through you. It is an open question whether this turning a deaf ear toward mother and, consequently, toward the outside world is inborn or an acquired defense. Their inability to use the symbiotic partner makes it necessary for these children to find substitutive adaptive mechanisms for survival, and these substantive formations represent the symptomatology of early infantile autism" (Mahler, 1979, p. 172).

In the case that will be described, in this chapter, the child often sought out reflective surfaces and would become totally absorbed in gazing at herself, even though she characteristically looked at other human beings with apparently nonseeing eyes. This preoccupation with her reflected image seemed to give her great pleasure. It is not unusual for these children to be captivated by their reflected image. One wonders whether an autistic child's fascination with mirrored reflections might be a substitute restitutive attempt to feel real, to affirm existence, to escape fragmentation and isolation, even though Mahler conceives of distance-perceptive visual images as a later development, less related to the creation of a body image, more related to a child's relationship to his object world.

Briefly, the second type of infantile psychoses that Mahler describes is symbiosis, which, in contrast to the isolation of the autistic child, is characterized by the loss of boundaries between self and object, between child and mother. So fused in the mother-child unity, such children are incapable of achieving the necessary stage of separation and individuation and instead react with catastrophic panic reactions at such a prospect. We will not dwell further on this pathological state in order to retain our focus on early infantile autism.

Mahler stress that the autistic infant does not perceive the mother emotionally; she remains a part object, indistinguishable from inanimate objects. The affective perception of other human beings is absent. Mahler recalled some of the comments mothers of such children have been heard to make: "He never greeted me." "She was never cuddly." "She did not want anyone to embrace her." "Never noticed when I left the room" (1979, p. 136). Such quotations are very similar to the ones made by the parents of the child to be discussed in this chapter. The inability of the autistic child to distinguish between inanimate and animate impairs the child's comprehension of the surrounding world, as well as his sense of identity. The loss or lack of this ability to discriminate between the living and the lifeless can evoke terrifying feelings. Mahler provided an excellent clinical example: One of her child patients was panic-stricken when he had to pass a certain picket fence for fear that the holes might swallow him (1979, p. 178). Mahler has also pointed out that the autistic child is irritated by any intrusion and characteristically will have a temper tantrum to fend intrusion. Again to quote Mahler:

"It would seem that autism is the basic defense attitude of these infants, for whom the beacon of emotional orientation in the outer world—the mother as primary love object—is nonexistent. Early infantile autism develops, I believe, because the infantile personality, devoid of emotional tied to the person of the mother, is unable to cope with external stimuli and inner excitations, which threaten from both sides his very existence as an entity. Autism is therefore the mechanism by which such patients try to shut out . . . the potential sources of sensory perception, particularly those which demand affective response" (1968, p. 69).

This brings to mind the research, discussed earlier, on the development of joint attention and/or intersubjectivity in the infant, which appears to be relatively absent in the autistic child, who is burdened instead with some form of emotional aphasia. Hobson (1990) suggests that without what Mahler terms a beacon of emotional orientation, such "children may become fixed in a restricted inflexible concrete mode of apprehending meanings, and remain limited in their understanding of meaning-conferring minds (including their own)" (p. 330).

In order to contrast Mahler's view of the etiological factors in infantile autism with behaviorist and other nonanalytic orientations, it is important to understand that she perceives the core deficiency in this disorder to lie in the child's inability to use the symbiotic object to gratify its needs. This incapacity impairs the development of the ego with regard to its integrating and organizing functions; it is "the primary cause for the psychotic fragmentation of the ego" (1968, p. 69). Other schools of thought center their attention on the child as the "carrier of the disease" (1979, p. 159). This has crucial implications for treatment. The nonanalytic approaches tend to minimize and/or bypass the importance of the child's contact with a human love object. They tend to concentrate on the cognitive and linguistic deficits or what appears to be a defect in the functioning of one or another of the sense organs (e.g., visual or auditory) in an effort to provide or improve those missing or defective faculties. Mahler, on the other hand, has emphasized that the first and primary goal in treatment is to lure the autistic child out of his shell into an object relationship. To quote Mahler, "Our first therapeutic endeavor . . . is to engage the child in a 'corrective symbiotic experience'" (1979, p. 224). "[He] must be kept from retreating into the autistic defensive position. He must be enticed and be encouraged to relive a more gratifying— albeit still regressive—exclusively symbiotic-parasitic relationship with a substitute mother" (1979, p. 231). She has cautioned, however, that the therapist must take care not to force such a child too rapidly into human contact —*Lure* is the operant term. Mahler has suggested using a variety of devices to achieve this goal: music, rhythmical activities, use of inanimate objects. But she was equally confident that the shell of the autistic child could be penetrated via the therapeutic relationship. We believe that our case presentation will attest to that conclusion. Mahler (1979), along with her colleagues Bergman and Furer, developed what they termed the tripartite treatment design. This approach includes the mother in the treatment sessions at the outset. In the presence of the mother the therapist lures the child out of its autistic state into a symbiotic attachment and then unites the mother and child in a corrective symbiotic experience. As the treatment progresses, the mother with the therapist even makes interpretations about the child's feelings and conflicts.

Like Mahler, Tustin (1981) also delineated two states of childhood psychoses: (1) the autistic reaction of encapsulation (she refers to children with such a disorder as shell-type children), and (2) the confusional type, which correlates closely with Mahler's description of symbiosis; we will not expand on the latter category. Like Mahler, Tustin views the autistic reaction as a defensive maneuver. As mentioned earlier, Mahler believed that because the autistic child does not have emotional ties to the mother and therefore cannot use her to ward off internal and external stimuli that "threaten . . . his very existence as an entity," autism is used to shut out sensory perceptions, especially those that might evoke an affective reaction. Tustin has described the rationale for the autistic defense somewhat differently. First and foremost, she stresses that it attempts to deal with "unmitigated terror" (1991, p. 585). Perhaps here she differs from Mahler only in her dramatic phraseology. But her focus on the trauma the infant experiences in becoming aware of his bodily separateness from the mother deviates from Mahler's thinking. In Tustin's words: "Austism can be seen as a massive 'not-knowing' and 'not-hearing' provoked by traumatic awareness of bodily separateness . . . separateness from a mother with whose body they had previously felt fused and equated. Prior to the alarmingly unexpected awareness of bodily separateness, they had not been aware of a mothering person, as such. They had taken her bodily presence for granted. They only realized that 'it' had been there when they felt that 'it' had gone. When awareness of their separateness was suddenly experienced, it was as if they had lost part of *their* body. This brought their vulnerability home to them. They felt unprotected and at risk. Autism became an impenetrable protection which shut out painful awareness" (1991, p. 586).

Tustin claims that autistic children are not fully born, that they still experience themselves as part of the mother's body. Existence for them is "fraught with danger" (1991, p. 586).

Tustin (1981, 1991) has interpreted the observed tendency of autistic children to become attached to small hard objects, which they insist upon holding tightly, in the light of her conceptual frame. According to Tustin, these hard objects are held tightly by these children because of the skin reactions they arouse. She believes that the sensations that these objects produce "distract attention from unbearable bodily separateness, and assuage the terrors which beset these children . . ." (1991, p. 588). She interprets other autistic behaviors similarly, for example, hand flapping, finger flicking, twirling.

In evaluating psychoanalytic writings, it would be well to heed Hobson's cautionary note, one he particularly sounds for Tustin's work. "Tustin's more elaborate formulations will need further analysis in relation to the autistic child's less articulated concepts of the forms and function of things, of bodies, and of people" (Hobson, 1990, p. 331). Hobson alerts us "to the danger of moving from our own representation of what children's experience is like to a conviction that this is how the children themselves represent such experience" (1990, p. 331).

We will now present our account of an autistic child, treated in psychoanalytically oriented psychotherapy. The title of our paper, "From Autism to Oedipus," has been drawn from the clinical material. Esther Fine has been the child therapist, and she describes a psychotherapeutic journey that begins with an autistic child and ends at a point where this same child is struggling with her oedipal problems.

CASE PRESENTATION

Mollie was 2¾ years when I (E. F.) first learned of her presenting difficulties. Her parents referred by the paternal grandmother who was very concerned about Mollie's strange behavior, particularly as it related to Mollie's seeming total disinterest in her, as well as other people in her family with the exception of the housekeeper and her mother. She also expressed concern about the fact that the child had little if any comprehensible speech. This latter fact disturbed her less, because Mollie's father had also been delayed in his speech development, and with speech therapy and psychotherapy he had developed normally, although he did have tantrums like Mollie.

Initially I met with Mollie's parents. While both parents participated in detailing Mollie's current problems and her history, the father seemed more concerned about the serious nature of the pathology. With sorrow he described how Mollie did not seem to be aware that he existed. He could come and go without any acknowledgment from Mollie. The parents thought that she might have a hearing deficit, but an examination revealed that there was no hearing loss.

Mollie for the most part had minimal contact with people. She used them like inanimate objects to open doors, to reach for something she was incapable of getting herself. Most of the time she had a nonseeing gaze that did not seem to perceive the world about her. She liked to put together puzzles. She could spend long periods of time doing the same puzzle over and over again. If she was interrupted in such a repetitive activity, she was likely to have a tantrum. She was also likely to have a tantrum when the mother left for work in the morning. She would awaken in the middle of the night and come into the parents' bedroom to crawl in bed with them. If they tried to return her to her bed, she became hysterical. The occasion where her tantrums were always predictable was at birthday parties, especially when the candles were blown out and "Happy Birthday" was sung.

The mother estimated that Mollie had approximately thirty words that she could identify. These words were barely comprehensible. The remainder of her verbalizations were a kind of babble.

While she often had a nonseeing gaze, she would look at herself in anything that provided a reflection of her—mirrors, windows, reflective metals.

She was not toilet trained and no attempt had been made to bring this about. Her primary caregiver was a Hispanic housekeeper who did not speak English. The caregiver was described by the parents and the grandmother as having dull intelligence. They also described her as being very indulgent with Mollie, giving her whatever she wanted; they claimed that she never had limits for Mollie.

Both parents work: the mother is a professional woman, whose workday begins very early in the morning and ends in the early evening. The father is a businessman whose hours are somewhat more flexible, but whose primary availability to his children is on weekends. Mollie has an older sister by two years. One-half year after this first meeting with the parents, the mother gave birth to her third child, a boy. These siblings showed no signs of autism. The housekeeper also had a child who is six years older than Mollie and who lives with the family; the parents consider this child as one of their own, and are responsible for her well-being and education. The mother stated that she spent a great deal of her free time helping this child with her homework, so much so that the older daughter felt neglected. Both parents admitted that neither of them spent very much time with Mollie. She seemed to prefer the maid to them or preferred to engage in her solitary, repetitive activities. She took little or no note of her sister or the housekeeper's daughter.

Mollie never derived comfort from transitional objects like soft, cuddly stuffed animals or a blanket. Instead, she would insist at times on holding a small hard metal toy or plastic object and would have a tantrum if it were misplaced.

Mollie had eating problems. The parents reported that she seemed to eat very little, and there were few foods that she was interested in eating. She would have tantrum if not given specifically what she wanted.

The mother reported that during her eighth month of pregnancy with Mollie, she was in a car accident. She was hit broadside on the driver's side, while driving. She wondered if that accident affected Mollie's development. Mollie's birth was eventful in that the umbilical cord was wrapped around her neck, although the mother stressed that this problem was easily rectified and that she was more likely to attribute any difficulties Mollie might have to the automobile accident.

The mother had wanted to breast-feed Mollie, and had taken a three-month leave of absence to be with her. However, Mollie had great difficulty in grasping and holding onto the nipple with her mouth. The father attempted to be helpful by holding Mollie's head. When Mollie opened her mouth, the father would push her head toward and into the mother's breast. Many times Mollie would fail to grasp the nipple; however, sometimes when she did, she would clamp down so hard that the mother would scream out in pain. The parents described this period as a nightmare. They continued this method for a brief period, then gave up, and Mollie was transferred to a bottle and primarily to the care of the housekeeper. After a couple months the mother returned to full-time work.

Further history was relatively sparse. As noted the paternal grandmother had complained that Mollie's development did not appear normal to her; it seemed slow. She did not walk until fifteen months of age. But the mother simply felt that every child has his or her idiosyncratic growth pattern. She had been confident that Mollie would be all right. Their pediatrician had also assured the parents of this.

My first meeting with the parents was held in December 1989. I recommended that Mollie be psychologically tested and evaluated at a local university, and I also suggested that I see Mollie three or four times for a clinical evaluation.

In my first meeting with Mollie, I found her to be a very pretty child with long, blonde, curly hair, blue eyes, and a beautifully formed body. But she also appeared like an autistic child, with some of the typical features that have been described: She had a vacant stare; she seemed for the most part oblivious of me and the office surroundings. When her mother brought her into the room, she brought Mollie's attention to some puzzles I had set out by dumping the pieces of one of the puzzles out and putting them together correctly. Mollie soon became absorbed in doing the puzzles over and over again. While she seemed quite adept at putting together these puzzles, there seemed to be something mechanical and nonseeing about the way she did it, almost robotic, even though she was very accurate.

I had also set a family of dolls around a toy dining room table. On some miniature plates, I rolled some Play-Doh. I wanted to see if I could engage her in some fantasy play. Autistic children are thought to be very limited, if not barren in their fantasy life. She continued repeatedly putting together the same puzzle. Then she reached over and put some of the play dough in her mouth. The mother cautioned her not to eat it. Mollie seemed not to hear her; then suddenly tried to put some play dough in her mother's mouth.

Her speech seemed incomprehensible babble. When she spoke, she was not addressing us, but rather seemed to be talking to herself. I noted what the parents had mentioned to me, namely that she would catch a reflection of herself in a window and behave as if she were carrying on a conversation with her mirrored image. She seemed to be pleased with what she saw reflected. At the same time she seemed oblivious of her mother and me.

The second time I saw Mollie her behavior was very similar to the first session. Her behavior was repetitive and had a stereotyped quality. At one point, however, she sat on her mother's lap and the mother engaged her in rhymes like "itsy, bitsy spider"; Mollie imitated the mother's gestures at the same time as she looked intensely into the mother's eyes, almost as if they were glued together. There was a kind of concentrated fusion with her mother that was distinctly different than her behaviors in which she seemed oblivious of her mother or me. The way they related to each other had a strange symbiotic quality.

In my third evaluative session Mollie did emerge briefly in some fantasy play. I had again placed some family dolls, which simulated her family, around the toy dining room table. She took the doll that might most likely represent her and placed her chair right next to the doll that represented the mother. She pretended to feed the mother doll, then again tried to put play dough in her mother's mouth as well as her own. But most of the time was spent as in the previous sessions, in putting together three puzzles, dumping them out and putting them together again in her characteristic repetitive fashion.

I concluded that Mollie indeed had certain autistic features. I again recommended testing to the parents if they wanted a more conclusive diagnosis. The parents wanted me to assure them that some form of treatment would be helpful to Mollie and that one day she would be normal. I felt that it was encouraging that she engaged in fantasy play, albeit very limited. I also thought it was a positive sign that she could show her attachment to her mother, even though, as already noted, it seemed to be a rather strange one, symbiotic in nature. I shared these thoughts with the parents, but they understood at this point that I could not guarantee normality.

I told the parents that if I were to take Mollie into treatment, I would want to see her frequently, no less than four times a week. They were agreeable to this arrangement. The local university was unable to give her an appointment earlier than two months from the time the parents contacted them. This appointment was set up, and in the meantime I proceeded to see Mollie four times a week for approximately fifty-minute sessions.

In the beginning her mother remained in the treatment room. If she got up to leave, Mollie had a tantrum. After about two weeks, however, Mollie accepted her mother sitting in the reception room with the door open to the playroom. By the third week she remained alone with me in the office.

In the two months before her psychological testing Mollie made considerable gains. The parents noted an almost immediate ability to relate to others. In her sessions with me she characteristically brought some hard object, which she would grasp in her hand, and if it was misplaced, she would begin to scream. She became increasingly involved in the fantasy play that involved placing her doll representative very close to the mother doll. Sometimes she would actually remove the father doll from the table as if she did not want him to be part of the family. She enjoyed feeding the mother doll play dough. She continued to put the play dough in her mouth, ignoring my limits regarding this. Most of the time in this period it seemed as if she did not see or hear me, although she would use me as one might use an inanimate object to secure what she wanted. She would take my hand and guide it to perform some act.

I felt as if I were trying to break through a wall that she had built around her. I initiated some peek-a-boo games to try and achieve this. These games were the first real contact I felt with Mollie. She would sometimes squeal with delight as I hid behind a chair and suddenly appeared again. Soon she was initiating the peek-a-boo game. The Eames chair on which we played the game was on a swivel, and when she discovered that fact she wanted me to turn her around on it. I verbally made a distinction for her as to when I was turning her around fast and when I was turning her around slowly. In fact I was verbalizing all our actions and feelings virtually nonstop. Somehow it seemed to me that it was instructive for her if I articulated everything I surmised was going on. I think it was my way of (1) keeping in constant touch with her; (2) communicating to her that our behaviors, our actions, and thoughts had verbal, symbolic representation; and (3) hoping that she would increasingly understand the meaning I was trying to convey to her about herself, her world, and our relationship. Many times, however, I would have to repeat her name several times before she would make eye contact with me, and, therefore, give me the impression that she was aware of my presence.

She would indicate to me that she wanted me to spin her around in the chair by pulling my hand and placing it on the chair. I said firmly that I would not turn her around unless she said: "Turn it around." She kept tugging at my hand, but I was firm in my determination that she was to verbalize this command. Finally, frankly to my great surprise, she said, "Turn it around." This was the first comprehensible verbal statement she had made. I telephoned her mother to apprise her of this. She was unbelieving until that same night she placed Mollie on a swivel chair and Mollie said it again. Next, with my encouragement, Mollie was able to distinctly tell me whether she wanted to be turned around slowly or "fast."

While Mollie continued to improve, long periods of time in our sessions contained clear remnants of her autistic-like behaviors. She continued in her repetitive, stereotyped activities of repeatedly doing the same puzzles with which she was familiar. She shunned the new ones. I also noted that she ignored any new toys or dolls in the office, until they had been there for several weeks.

She continued to attend to the dolls around the toy dining table. I would name them and verbally give meaning to Mollie's activity with them. If she fed the mother, I might comment that Mollie was feeding her mother the way she would like to be fed by her mother. If she removed the father doll and hid him away, I would point out that she did not seem to want him around, maybe to have mother all for herself. Other times she would include the father, and that seemed to be a positive sign in her relationship with him; indeed the father reported that his relationship with Mollie was improving, that she now seemed to be aware of him and more encouraging, actually seemed to enjoy him.

It became increasingly clear that Mollie looked forward to seeing me. The parents reported that she would sometimes have a tantrum when she thought she was coming to see me and they would turn the car in a direction that was clearly not taking her to my office. At this early phase in the treatment, Mollie's speech was still an incomprehensible babble for the most part. She was still putting Play-Doh in her mouth. She continued to bring hard objects and throw tantrums if they were misplaced, particularly at home.

I placed a basket filled with little raisin boxes, hoping she would select them instead of placing play dough in her mouth. In fact, I told her raisins were to eat and play dough was to pretend eating. And indeed finally she made the shift. One day she placed a raisin on her upper front teeth. I then took a raisin and placed it on my front teeth, said "Stick," and pressed my finger against the raisin. Then I said in a singsong voice, "You and me, eating raisins, yum, yum, yum, yum, yum." Mollie joined me, and this act was repeated over and over again for many weeks. Mollie seemed to get great pleasure from this activity. She would rock gently almost touching my head, and she would clearly pronounce the words as we rhythmically repeated them. I had a rationale in introducing this game. Mollie had an extremely difficult time in her earliest nursing experience with her mother; she could not connect with her. I hypothesized that it might be therapeutic for Mollie to symbolically repeat this experience, this time successfully. It clearly became very important to Mollie to play this game. She would initiate it frequently and seemed to experience great joy and connectedness with me at the time. Her enunciation of the words was the clearest yet.

The raisin game led to other games in which we either did them together or I was to initiate her or she, me. These activities might involve naming and pointing our fingers at different parts of our face and body; it might involve jumping up and down or playing patty-cake, or marching and following the leader.

Mollie also discovered my soft stuffed-animal puppets. She almost always gave me the giraffes and took a little kitten for herself. She thoroughly enjoyed having the giraffes hug the kitten. Sometimes she had them all join in ring-around-a-rosie.

Two months had passed, and Mollie was scheduled for a full battery of psychological testing at the university's center for the study of autistic children. Briefly, the tests indicated that Mollie was a high-functioning autistic child, who demonstrated classical signs of autism. To quote from these reports:

> The following behaviors were noted: body rocking, grimacing, gesticulation, playing in the mirror, leading the adult by the hand, lining up objects, and hand flapping. . . . Otherwise behavior problems noted: is overly dependent, is withdrawn, is in diapers, does not eat, has a sleeping problem (has difficulty falling asleep and wakes up during the night), avoids work, cries or laughs too easily, has poor eye contact, sometimes seems excessively unhappy, has poor concentration and attention except when she is interested, has temper tantrums, which can last up to forty minutes, runs away, is stubborn, has excessive or peculiar preoccupations, says things that do not make sense, has peculiar mannerisms (such as hand flapping) uses bizarre speech and is unaware of what's happening around her.

The reports concluded, and again I quote: "(Mollie) is a 2-year, 10-month-old child, who presents with a history, behaviors on examination, and a patterning of skills on cognitive tests which would be consistent with the diagnosis of the syndrome of autism (DSM-III-R, 299.0). At this point in time (Mollie's) behavior interferes with an accurate assessment of her intellectual potential."

The specialists involved in her testing and evaluation strongly recommended that she be hospitalized at their center for a minimum of thirty days. The parents would be able to visit at designated times during the evenings. The parents were informed that autistic children do not suffer from separation anxiety, and therefore, the hospitalization would have no deleterious effects. She would be subjected to a structured regime, in which behavioral modification techniques would be used. The parents were told that psychotherapy had no value for autistic children. I would not be permitted to see Mollie while she was in the hospital, because such visits would be viewed as interfering with their treatment plan.

The parents were deeply concerned about these recommendations. They consulted me as to whether the suggested treatment plan would be helpful and appropriate for Mollie. I told them that I believed that Mollie did indeed suffer from separation anxiety, and in fact some of her autistic behavior was more than likely her strategy for coping with such anxiety. I made it very clear that I was opposed to hospitalization; indeed, I was fearful that it might worsen Mollie's condition. The parents decided to take my advice, and Mollie has continued in her therapy four times weekly. The parents were also seen on a regular basis—at first every two weeks and now every three or four weeks. We also have telephone contact on an as-needed basis. They inform me about all that is going on in Mollie's life, and I give them a rather detailed account of what I believe will be helpful for them to know about Mollie's sessions with me.

At the end of six months of treatment, Mollie demonstrated considerable progress in her ability to relate to me. She had begun to form a very close bond with me. She began to greet me joyously, when I would open the door to the reception room upon her arrival. She called me Estherhouse, a contraction based on the fact that her parents would tell her before coming to my office that they were going to Esther's house. In fact, she called me by this name during the first two years of therapy. Her eye contact vastly improved. She appeared to be actually seeking out eye contact with me, even turning her head backwards in order to continue gazing at me.

Her speech improved. As she began to communicate verbally, her beginning speech was characterized by echolalia and almost incomprehensible babble where only an occasional word was recognizable. I noted that she imitated my voice inflections and my tone of voice. She began her real progress in verbal communications by giving commands. The clarity of her speech would vary from remarkably clear to almost incomprehensible. There were still occasions when her speech seemed to be pure babbling. In the sixth month she expanded her one-word commands to two words, which seemingly gave her a great sense of power and control over me. "Stand up!"; "Sit down!"; "Go down!"; "Play rosie!" (referring to ring-around-a-rosie). In addition she began for the first time to use full sentences. She also began to use personal possessive pronouns, although she would confuse them, as autistic children tend to do.

At this point in the treatment, Mollie still showed many autistic features, despite her marked improvement. While there were occasional instances of spontaneous playfulness, much of her behavior was ritualistic, repetitive, and stereotyped. She was clearly fearful of the unfamiliar. Each time a new book appeared in my office, she would toss it away as if she could not tolerate the presence of something new. She would urge me to read one of the older books with which she was very familiar. Gradually, and with trepidation, she would permit herself to show interest in the new book after she had seen it in the office a few times. She showed signs of handling her anxiety with autistic withdrawal; for example, during this sixth month of treatment a baby brother was born. She behaved as if she were oblivious to him. Once the mother brought the baby to the reception room, and his screaming penetrated into the office. Mollie behaved as if she heard nothing. When I commented on it, she behaved as if *I* had said nothing.

I mentioned earlier that Mollie was not toilet trained when she began treatment. And the parents, for their part, had not as yet been able to help her accomplish this. Now it became imperative that she be trained, not only because of the birth of the new baby, but because the parents wanted to enroll her in a preschool that might not accept her if she were not toilet trained. I purchased a few picture books on potty training, but except for one, which required playful manipulation, she was not interested in them. What was significant about this period was that Mollie became very involved in paints and water. She particularly liked to engage in smearing the paints—even smearing her face and her tongue. She interspersed this particular play with placing the mother doll with the doll representing herself on what she called the daddy horse. I thought at the time that she was creating a bond between her parents and herself, while simultaneously expressing anger toward them and the new baby by smearing paint. Also Mollie might have found it helpful to sublimate wishes to smear and play with feces by playing with paint and water. In any case, Mollie became toilet trained relatively easily and entered a preschool class for autistic and developmentally impaired children.

After the birth of her brother, Mollie showed no overt hostility toward him, but her mother reported that Mollie distanced herself from the mother. Her tantrums during this period increased. In her sessions with me she often threw the baby doll away before beginning her fantasy play. Then she would place the mother and father doll on a horse together with the doll that represented herself. After a month or two of this, she began to include the baby doll, seemingly reflective of a beginning acceptance of the new baby in her house. "No!" had become a prominent word in her vocabulary, and when I asked her if the baby wasn't too young to ride on a horse with her, she responded with a resounding "No!"

Mollie's play tended to be brief and flitting. Her fantasies usually included a family of dolls: mother, father, housekeeper, but no older sister. At the time that she began to include the baby in her fantasies, she sought out face makeup and was clearly trying to make up her face as she had seen her mother do.

Next Mollie entered into a phase in which she repeatedly had me paint ice cream cones of different colors. I suspected that it related to the fact that her mother was nursing her baby brother, and it involved my providing her with a symbolic breast.

In her fantasies about her trips with her family, Mollie provided me with clues as to who was disturbing her; for she would purposely include or exclude certain family members on such trips.

Mollie began to show increasing affection toward me. It became a customary act for her to climb on my lap and put her arms around my neck sometime during our session.

Mollie introduced a new topic into her fantasy play: the birthday party. One of Mollie's presenting problems, and one that had persisted, was her tendency to have tantrums at birthday parties. As was my custom in treating Mollie, when she indicated an area of conflict or disturbance, I would purchase children's books that related to that subject, as a way of communicating with this verbally limited child. I did so in the case of her interest in birthday parties. She was not only interested in certain of these books, but she created her own repetitive play, which covered many sessions. She made a birthday cake out of play dough; she placed three candles on it and then proceeded to sing "Happy Birthday" to herself. She would characteristically be very pleased with herself; she clearly enjoyed being the special birthday girl. The repetitive birthday theme continued for the next six months, appearing in nearly every session, and although it was to reappear later usually in connection with the birthday of a family member or a friend, it has not assumed the central importance that it did in this period. Various aspects of her conflict regarding birthdays were taken up: her need to feel special, her feeling that others were in the spotlight instead of her, arousing her envy and her feelings of being neglected, her anxiety that she would be denied her infantile needs if she got older. After this six-month phase focused on issues relating to her birthday, the mother reported that Mollie stopped having tantrums at birthday parties, a major relief for the entire family.

Signs of Mollie's autism continued to appear especially when her separation anxiety was aroused. In the eighth month of treatment the mother was twenty minutes late in picking her up. Mollie withdrew and stared blankly. With considerable effort I was able to bring her out of this autistic state. Connected with this type of reaction was Mollie's way of departing from me. She would not say good-bye to me, despite her parents and her grandmother's many efforts to get her to do so. Finally I said to her grandmother, who was instructing Mollie to say goodbye: "Hello is much easier for Mollie than good-bye"; whereupon Mollie mischievously said "Good-bye!" By the ninth month of treatment she began to master her anxiety and distress over leaving her session. She would repeat my phrase, "See you tomorrow" or "See you Friday," until she was saying it without my initiating it.

In the ninth month of treatment Mollie began carrying a whole armful of stuffed animals with her everywhere she went. This began at a time when her parents were on vacation. When they returned, the beloved housekeeper and the paternal grandmother both went on vacation. And to add insult to injury, the father again left on a trip. In a session with me she placed the mother doll and the doll who represented the housekeeper on a horse together and pranced the horse as if it were taking them away. She pretended to cry. She tried to place all her animals on another toy horse. I enacted a scene for Mollie and she seemed fascinated. I spoke for the Mollie doll: "Don't go bye-bye. It makes me sad. I want all the animals with me to protect me because Mommy and Daddy and Consuelo and Grandma went away." When Mollie rejoined her mother at the end of the session, I explained to the mother in front of Mollie in language that Mollie would understand why it was necessary for Mollie to carry with her all her stuffed animals. Mollie listened attentively and gave me a bright smile. Shortly after this session the mother contacted me to tell me that Mollie stopped insisting that all her stuffed animals accompany her wherever she went.

After a year of treatment Mollie's autistic behavior diminished considerably. She became much more outgoing and friendly, especially with her peers and teacher in her preschool. She was clearly the most verbal child in the class. I observed her there one day.

As I mentioned before, I would select children's books that related to problems that Mollie seemed to be dealing with: sibling rivalry, the new baby, sleeping problems, eating problems, problems in playing with peers: sharing, rejection. I noted that she was identifying letters and occasionally words, so I began to teach her to read and she gave indications that she was learning. In the first grade, she tested in reading at the third grade level. She spoke in full sentences, and no longer mixed up her pronouns. While her speech is now very comprehensible, there is occasionally a kind of mechanical, stilted quality about the way she speaks, although this is disappearing.

At four-and-a-half to five years of age Mollie began to introduce her fantasies with more forcefulness. She had watched *The Jungle Book* on video and became obsessed with it. She pretended to be Mowgli, the man-cub, the boy raised by wolves, a leopard, and a bear. She assigned me the role of Baloo, the bear that watched over Mowgli. She repeatedly encountered danger from wild animals and would leap screaming in terror into my arms for protection. She repeated this play many times in many sessions. There certainly seemed to be a parallel between the terror experienced by Mowgli in facing the wild beasts of the jungle and the terror Mollie seemed to experience in her world when her tantrums became out of control. She turned to me as if I provided a safe harbor for her.

Mollie was entering her third year in treatment. About this time, the mother called to report that Mollie was biting people—her sister, brother, even a teacher at school. She hoped that I could understand this new problem, so that I could help Mollie with it. When I directly confronted Mollie with her biting, she vehemently denied it. I think, however, that the material that I am about to describe to you sheds light on it. Mollie had shown a great deal of interest in the story of Beauty and the Beast. It began by her simply saying "Beauty and the Beast" to let me know she had seen the movie. I explained to her that when Beauty said "I love you" to the Beast, he turned into a handsome prince. We alternated playing Beauty and the Beast. Mollie as the Beauty would say "I love you," and I as the Beast would lose my ugly grimace, which I had assumed. This fantasy was replayed many times during the course of the next month.

Mollie shifted to using the Ken and Barbie dolls to represent Beauty and the Beast. She would have them marry and dance together. She instructed me to make a beast of the Ken doll's face, which I did by wrapping a paper towel around his head, drawing a beast's face and securing it with a rubber band. Mollie would pull the paper mask off after she, speaking for Beauty, would say "I love you" and "Now you are a handsome prince."

In one of the many sessions in which Mollie played out this fantasy, she noted some actual scratches on the Barbie doll's leg. She told me that Mommy had bitten her—her first reference to biting. In a following session she again noted the scratches and again told me that Mommy bit her. She faced off the Barbie doll representing Beauty and the one representing Mommy and speaking for Beauty, she said "Mommy, you bitch! Don't bite me anymore." I asked why Mommy bit her. She replied: "She wants to dance with daddy. Mommy can dance with Uncle P" (using the name of her mother's brother). She had two sets of Ken and Barbie dolls dance together, while she sang "Beauty and the Beast," the title song from the picture. One set represented the mommy and Uncle P and the other Beauty and the Beast. I spoke for the mommy. I said "No, Daddy is *my* husband. He should dance with me." "Dance with Uncle P," she ordered. In a more conciliatory tone, she said: "Mommy *wants* to dance with Uncle P. I said "I know that you want Daddy all for yourself. You *want* to think Mommy wants to dance with Uncle P." I added: "Beauty, when you grow up, you will have your own prince. Daddy is *my* husband!" To this Mollie responded: "Mollie is growing up, I am getting bigger."

The oedipal theme that Mollie introduced through her fantasies about the Beauty and the Beast was played out in different variations. Clearly, her competition with her mother for her father was being depicted in these fantasies. Her tendency to bite diminished. I thought that she was beginning to resolve this conflict; I had high hopes at the beginning of the session I am about to describe.

Mollie was brought this day by her father. As I opened the door to the reception room, she said: "This is my best friend, Daddy." Mollie had brought a new Barbie doll with her. She took out my Barbie and Ken dolls. She placed my Ken and Barbie doll who usually represented the chosen couple (i.e., Beauty and the Beast) together. She placed her Barbie, which I suspected represented herself, with the Ken doll that stood for Uncle P. She had each respective couple kiss each other." They are going to get married," she told me. She sang "Here comes the bride," very sweetly. She pronounced each couple man and wife, then placed each couple on a bed. She assigned me the roles of Beauty and the Beast, while she acted out Barbie and Uncle P. As Beauty I reminisced with my prince. I said, "Remember when Barbie wanted you to be her prince. She bit me on the leg, because she was so angry with me." Mollie responded, "I'm sorry, Belle. Thank you, Prince, for making it better. I was a little girl then. I'm a grown-up lady now. I have my own prince." She had each couple dance together; Mollie sang a cheerful accompaniment: "I Could Have Danced All Night" from *My Fair Lady*. Suddenly, in a commanding voice, she said: "Switch!" And she exchanged the prince and Uncle P dolls, so that her Barbie doll now had the prince. I spoke as Beauty: "So you wanted my prince all for yourself all the time." She retorted with a resounding "Yes!" I continued: "But I told you, even though my prince loves you, he is *my* prince. You'll have to find your own prince when you grow up!" She repeated, "I was a little girl. I'm grown-up now. I have my own prince."

She interrupted this fantasy play by saying: "Now I am Mollie and you are Esther. Let's play *West Side Story*." We became in the new fantasy the star-crossed lovers. She was Maria and I was assigned the role of Tony. She happily sang the romantic songs from the musical: "I Feel Pretty," "Tonight," and "Maria." I noted that she picked up a spool of thread and held it tightly in one hand. It was the only clue I picked up that she was under tension. I asked her if the spool made her feel protected because this story had an unhappy ending. "No!" she said. "This spool protects me against Ursula." I knew that Ursula was the witch in *The Little Mermaid* who attempts to interfere with the Little Mermaid marrying Prince Eric. "Oh," I countered, "You were afraid Ursula would be angry, because she doesn't want you to have the prince." "Yes!" she agreed. Then she resumed playing out the romantic relationship between Maria and Tony. Finally she ended this sequence by announcing that I was again Esther and she, Mollie. I might mention that this was the last time I observed Mollie clutching a small, hard object.

In sessions following she continued to play out oedipal themes. I want to report another one. Mollie entered my office this day clearly pleased to show me her new Barbie doll, a replica of Belle from the movie *Beauty and the Beast*. She pulled out my Barbie doll that she had previously used to represent Belle and said we were to play with two Belles and that each would have their own prince. Then she took out another of my Barbie dolls, one with very tangled hair —messed up by another child patient. She told me that this doll was Aurora, and she was a witch. Mollie proceeded to have the three Barbies kiss each other in loving friendship. I expressed surprise and wondered aloud how the Belles could be friendly with Aurora the Witch. Mollie informed me that it was because they both had their own prince now, so Aurora cannot take their prince away. That's why they can all be friends now." Mollie responded with an enthusiastic "Yes!" I thought that Mollie had resolved this age-old rivalry problem very well. Of course it has continued to rear its head.

Much of this time it was difficult to discern that Mollie was an autistic child. But there are lapses into autism. The parents hired a driver, usually a college-aged young woman, to bring Mollie to her therapy sessions. Once, the driver forcefully tried to engage me in conversation in order to obtain some information. It deprived Mollie of her usual enthusiastic greeting and hug. Mollie came into my office, seemingly totally oblivious of me. She sat down and started to read a book. When I addressed her, she behaved as if she had heard nothing. Next she lay down on the couch and stared vacantly. "Mollie," I insisted, "What is the matter?" I showed great emotion, which seemed to reach Mollie. I felt I was drawing her back from another world. "Are you angry that I talked to G?" No response. Finally she said to me: "When I was a little girl, I had a nightmare." I, of course, asked her what it was. She told me she dreamt she was a ballerina; she was chased by lions and bears and fell through a hole. I recognized that this dream was a variation on a dream recounted in one of the Berenstain bears stories. But Mollie had a different ending. She said that she fell into my lap. And to demonstrate, she jumped into my lap and all was well between us. I thought it was Mollie's way of telling me that when she feels disconnected from me, she enters a dangerous world of terror. But she also knows that I am there for her and I can give her a sense of security.

At age five and a half, Mollie entered a public school kindergarten, as part of the school's full inclusion program. She was previously in a preschool for autistic and other developmentally delayed children. She adjusted fairly well in kindergarten, although she had tantrums when she felt neglected or ignored. At this writing she has just entered first grade. The initial adjustment has been difficult for her, specifically in less structured situations again when she seemed to feel lost or ignored. Mollie still had tantrums, particularly in new, unfamiliar situations. The tantrums of today are short-lived, however, and far more easily controlled by reasoning or limit-setting. Her teacher has reported that Mollie does well in small groups, in structured situations when her attention can be focused on a specific task, and particularly when the teacher can work with her in a one-on-one relationship. However, in a large, unstructured group given over to free play, she has been known to become easily distressed, have emotional outbursts, and/or to withdraw by isolating herself from the group to read a book.

Recall that at the outset of treatment, Mollie had serious eating problems; they have virtually disappeared. She has a good appetite now, is mindful of eating healthy foods, and has acquired appropriate table manners.

With regard to her speech, I have noted that, while Mollie will use phrases and sentences very appropriately, they are at times exact replicas of statements made by some of her favorite story-book characters, giving her speech, at such times, a quality of sophisticated echolalia.

There is also a greater tendency toward repetitive play than is usually found in normal or neurotic children her age, but she is increasingly more spontaneous in her play. She has made friends at school, with whom she has play dates. She alternates having a crush on one or two boys in her class and has stated that she plans to marry one or the other when she grows up.

Mollie was six years old, and her fantasies were much more sophisticated and reality-bound. The following is an example.

Mollie entered my office this day with a great show of enthusiasm. She had brought with her a new Barbie doll and a pink teddy bear. She told me that she was going to name this doll Coretta. I asked how she came to think of this name, and she informed me that it was the name of Martin Luther King's wife. For her fantasy she used my dolls—two representing teenaged boys, both to be named Kevin and two others, a teenage girl and an eight- or ten-year-old girl, to be named Skipper and Stacy. The Kevin boys were to be the girls' boyfriends. Mollie spoke for the dolls. Kevin addressed Skipper: "What do you want to be when you grow up?" Skipper's answer was, "A rock star." Kevin said that he wanted to be an actor. They decided that they would each be both—a rock star and an actor.

They conceived of the idea of putting on a play—*Rumpelstiltskin.* Mollie had memorized the dialogue from the story. Kevin would be the woodsman and Skipper would be, to quote Mollie, "the miller's daughter who becomes a princess or a queen." She had the other set of dolls (Kevin and Stacy) perform the play too.

After the performances, the two couples decided to have a double wedding—a pretend wedding, because they were all too young to really get married. The ceremony closely followed accepted traditions. Afterwards, they all quickly changed from their bridal outfits to their resort clothes and took off for their respective honeymoons.

It would seem that the residuals of the oedipal conflicts are now expressed in peer relationships. Perhaps, Mollie resolves her sibling rivalry related to this issue by providing boyfriends with the same name to each of the girls in her story. In any case I submit that Mollie and I have indeed embarked on a journey from autism to Oedipus.

Discussion

The authors believe that the primary catalytic agent in the treatment of this autistic child was the formation of a corrective symbiotic experience, epitomized by the raisin game. Mollie was "lured" out of her autistic shell into gratifying human contact and connectedness.

Mollie was seen in individual psychotherapy. From the beginning, however, the parents were seen regularly; there was also telephone contact on an as-needed basis. The parents informed the therapist about what was going on in Mollie's life, and the therapist provided an account of what was deemed helpful for them to know about Mollie's sessions. Except for the first three weeks, however, the mother was not included in Mollie's therapy sessions. Therefore, the question can be raised as to whether Mahler and Bergman's tripartite treatment approach would have led to a more effective corrective symbiotic experience. In order to respond to the issue, it is important to consider factors unique to Mollie's case. Mollie had alternating autistic and symbiotic relationship to the mother. Recall that in the first session she put play dough in the mother's mouth, even though most of the time was spent in autistic withdrawal. Erna Furman, who discussed this case at a workshop of the Association for Child Psychoanalysis, expressed this idea very well: "(Mollie) was saying 'I am stuck at the point where I can still go either way.'" To have included the mother in the therapy room with the child would have likely created inordinate rivalry problems. Recall how in the second session she placed the doll representing herself very close to the mother and in subsequent hours repeated this act while throwing away her rivals (her father, her siblings). The child wanted to get rid of anyone who was connected with the mother. We think that if the mother had been permitted to stay, Mollie would have been more prone to view her therapist as an enemy who interfered with her symbiotic tie to the mother. We believe that the mother's relationship to Mollie improved by displacement through Mollie's developing progressive relationship to her therapist, which went through autistic, symbiotic, and then more mature phases of object relations. She was not so stuck in the symbiotic phase in her therapy. The therapist was neither the object of the disappointment and anger she harbored against the mother in some primitive form nor the great anxiety that her mother aroused when she would leave. In a sense the therapist served as a new object. We suspect that the father was rejected so completely at the beginning because he indeed was viewed as a threat to Mollie's symbiotic tie to the mother. Her fantasies captured the movement from symbiosis to freer and more expanded object relations, as the father and siblings were included in her fantasy play in a positive fashion. The father became a beloved and special person for her. In this period the mother became pregnant with her third child, and Mollie seemed to prepare herself for this event by increasing her distance from her mother and turning more to her father. The appearance of the oedipal attachment created a honeymoon period for Mollie and her father, while Mollie's rage toward the mother began to surface more directly. More recently Mollie has shifted her libidinal investments to one of two boys in her classroom, and she alternates between having a crush on one or the other.

Mollie's relationship to her parents has vastly improved. Both parents are very proud of her and view her progress as remarkable. She has tantrums at times; on occasion she will bite, particularly in rivalrous disputes with her siblings; so there still remain primitive expressions of her aggression and rage. But she also speaks directly about her anger toward her parents: she complains that they take too many vacations without her and they are too busy with their work. She can also express her love for them and demonstrate it in loving affection.

Would Mollie's therapy have had a better outcome had the mother been included in the therapy room? We think not. In our workshop discussion, Erna Furman made the point that "autistic children are not a group. They are as different as all other children are different." And it is in the light of these differences that one must tailor the treatment approach.

At the core of Mollie's fears and anxieties lay severe and primitive separation anxiety. The therapeutic relationship was established with Mollie when the peek-a-boo game was initiated—a game she came to love and played eagerly. As is well known, the peek-a-boo game is a child's method of restoring the love object, helping it to deal with separation anxiety. We suspect that doing the same puzzle over and over again in robotic fashion was a kind of peek-a-boo game for Mollie. She made figures disappear by dumping the puzzle pieces out of their form and then reappear by putting them together again. The therapist repeatedly reappeared when she spun her around on the swivel chair. Mollie took delight in catching glimpses of herself in anything that might reflect her image. This seemed to reassure her that she existed, that she had not disappeared. As related in the clinical presentation, Mollie worked with many issues connected to her disturbance about birthday parties. But in the context of her repeated attempts to master separation, loss, and annihilation, it is conceivable that the sudden disappearance of candlelight, when candles were blown out, evoked the unbearable anxiety of separation and annihilation.

Our differences with other psychoanalytic approaches to autism are relatively minor. Mahler, Bergman, Tustin, Furman, and others have all contributed to our thinking about this case. Our primary concern has been with the current trend in the literature about autism to negate the value of psychoanalysis, for it is clear to us, and hopefully to our readers, that the psychoanalytic perspective indeed provides an illuminating framework with which to view and treat the disorder of early infantile autism. Unfortunately there is little written of late in the psychoanalytic literature about this important subject matter. Susan Shersow's paper, published in February 2011, is one of the few articles that have been written. She advocates having the mother present in the child's therapy sessions and clearly from the discussion in this chapter on autism, I disagree.

The next chapter takes up a currently popular diagnosis ADHD, far less difficult to treat than autism.

Chapter Seven

ADHD

There has been an increasing tendency to treat many emotional disturbances with psycho-pharmacology. Neuroscience has made major advances in understanding the relationship between the functioning of the brain, the biochemistry of the nervous system and psychic phenomena, and it has contributed immensely to the development of medications that have benefited the mentally ill. However, it has also encouraged the illusion of the "quick fix." Unfortunately there is now a prevalent notion that it is no longer necessary or relevant to understand the unconscious meaning of psychological symptoms.

I found that the etiology of ADHD is a "hot issue" in the psychiatric and psychological literature, with the majority of papers favoring a neurological basis for the disorder. In my review of the psychoanalytic literature on ADHD, there was scant reference to this subject matter. Interestingly enough, I came across a heated debate on the American Psychoanalytic Association's website between two child analysts, Elio Frattaroli and Donald Rauh. Rauh had objected to a passage in a paper written by Paul Brinich. Rauh claimed it was irresponsible and uninformed, because Brinich claimed, and, I quote, "There is no clear-cut brain pathology and dysfunction associated with ADHD." Brinich also stated: "ADHD is a descriptive label used to summarize the fact that a substantial minority of our children have trouble 'staying between the lines, 'behaviorally speaking.'" The issue in question was a study by NIH, which, according to Rauh, "clearly demonstrated that there are differences in brain structure between those with and without ADHD; the cerebellar vermis is one of the structures involved and there are differences in overall brain size."

Frattaroli countered that such a difference in gross brain structure is not proof of a neurological cause for ADHD nor is the idea that there must be a neurological disease because Ritalin works. He also noted how many of the "scientific studies" that show the effectiveness of Ritalin have been financed by the drug companies.

Frattaroli also cited a study conducted by Laurence Greenhill of Columbia University that involved several hundred children from ages three to five who were thoroughly screened and diagnosed with ADHD. The purpose of the study was to determine the efficacy and safety of stimulants in very young children. Unlike studies financed by the drug companies, this study required the families in the study to participate in a behavioral intervention program before their children received Ritalin or a placebo. The outcome of the study was seriously compromised when nearly half the families opted out of the study after participating in the three-month intervention program. The parents were satisfied with the changes in their children. The researchers at this point no longer had a large enough sample to proceed with the study.

There are analysts who agree with Rauh. Allan Rosenblatt cited "several cases, in which, after several years of unsuccessful analysis, the addition of stimulant medication produced a prompt and striking improvement in their functioning." Rothstein (1998) too stressed the importance of recognizing the contribution of neurological dysfunction to patients diagnosed with ADHD. On the other hand, Peter Fonagy conducted a study of the efficacy of psychoanalysis for children with disruptive disorders, using a sample of 135 children. For those ADHD children who remained in treatment for more than one year. 67 percent were undiagnosable.

I see children in psychoanalytic psychotherapy, and frankly, it has been of deep concern to me to note the alacrity with which parents, teachers, and pediatricians medicate children to solve their emotional problems. The diagnosis of Attention Deficit/Hyperactivity Disorder is especially a case in point. It is not uncommon for a schoolteacher to inform parents that their child, unruly and difficult to handle in the classroom, is likely to have some form of attention deficit and might profit from medication (Montero, 2002). Parents then consult with their pediatrician, who too often complies with their request for medication, when that might not be the treatment of choice. In this paper I will illustrate such a case. This is not to suggest that there are no children who suffer from ADHD, that there is never a neurological basis for the disorder, or that stimulants like Ritalin, Adderall, or the non-stimulant Strattera are never helpful in the treatment of such children; however, in my experience it is overdiagnosed and overmedicated. In this clinical presentation I hope to underscore the multitude of determinants that can contribute to a child's problematic behavior in school and at home.

Seven-year-old Denny was referred for treatment because he was extremely disruptive, hyperactive, and uncooperative in school. He refused to listen to the teacher, he fought with the other children, and he was unable to follow through with a task. The only time he would follow directions was when the teacher became very angry with him. He had been having this difficulty since kindergarten and, halfway through the first grade, he was asked to leave public school. He was then enrolled in a private school but manifested the same behavioral difficulties there. The teacher informed his parents that she believed he had an attention deficit disorder and perhaps a medication like Ritalin would be helpful. She recommended that they discuss this matter with their pediatrician. The pediatrician did prescribe Ritalin, and when I saw Denny he had been on a course of this medication for about two months. As the private school was now considering expelling him, the parents sought psychotherapeutic help for their child.

I met initially with Denny's parents who provided a more detailed description of the child's presenting problems and his developmental history. Denny was the oldest of three boys; he had a brother who was six and another, four, when he began therapy. He had a very competitive relationship with these two brothers. He deeply resented it when they played with any of his toys, and he appeared to be rather obsessed with keeping his toys in a very special order. Whereas the mother emphasized his more violent nature, she made little mention of the fact that he was a very frightened child, overly sensitive to the slightest noises. This was apparent early in my work with him. He would always bring my attention to a fire engine or ambulance siren. He was quick to suspect an accident had occurred and, incidentally with good reason: both parents were very accident-prone; both had been involved in very serious auto accidents in which they were injured.

The father had an explosive rage; he had beaten his wife on several occasions. When she was eight months pregnant with Denny, he socked her in the stomach and split open her lip. When Denny was about 2½, he beat her so badly that she called the police. In the two years prior to their coming to therapy, the father had been much less likely to resort to physical violence; but the parents continued to have frequent verbal battles, mostly over sexual matters. The mother told me that she refrained from having sexual intercourse with her husband because he had been so brutal to her.

Developmental history: Denny's birth and very early infancy were described as normal. However, when he was eight months of age, he suffered from severe diarrhea and dehydration and was hospitalized for over a week at this time. He was tied down to the bed and fed intravenously. When he returned from the hospital, he was very frightened of anyone wearing white; in fact, he refused to go to his mother when she wore white.

The toilet training period was exceedingly difficult. Both parents were furious with Denny because he resisted toilet training. The father would check him every morning and hit him in the head when he found that Denny had wet or soiled. The mother, too, was extremely impatient and frequently slapped him for soiling. She said that she could not tolerate his saying no to her and would flick her long fingernails on his chin whenever he said this. She proudly reported that she had conditioned him in this way never to say no to her. The father continued hitting Denny for his bedwetting until the child was five, at which time Denny stopped wetting his bed. However, it was at this time that he started school and seemed to transfer much of his disturbance to the school situation.

Both parents had fathers who behaved toward them as they behaved with Denny. The father's father beat him severely when he did not do something right the first time. On occasion, he would actually pick him up and fling him against the wall, according to the father's account. Denny's father had hung up a placard in their home with a motto which read: "If you can't do it right the first time, what makes you think you can do it the second time?" Understandably, Denny had become very disturbed when he could not get something right the first time.

One of my first acts as Denny's therapist was to recommend that he be taken off Ritalin. I was given permission to consult with his pediatrician and he complied with my request. It seemed quite clear to me that this child had been severely traumatized during his brief lifetime, and this accounted for his emotional and behavioral difficulties rather than some form of brain dysfunction.

I saw Denny twice weekly and met with his parents every two to three weeks. In my work with the parents, we focused primarily on their parenting roles in an attempt to help them understand Denny and their relationship to him. We looked at the fact that they had treated Denny the way they had been treated as children.

Although the presenting complaints about Denny involved his tantrums, his defiance, his provocative behavior, I saw little evidence of it in his sessions with me, except later in his fantasy play. In fact, especially at the beginning, his demeanor was rather stiff and overly contained, possibly due to the medication, although he became progressively more relaxed. His approach to the toys and to his drawings was a careful, almost rigid, one. He would take great pains to set up the doll furniture exactly in place before he played out a fantasy. His drawings were also somewhat stiff and cautiously executed. However, once he became involved in a fantasy, his stiffness would fade away and his imagination would be given free rein. The second time I saw him, he made a painting which beautifully symbolized his relationship with his parents, particularly his mother. He drew a cactus with many thorns on it, but at the end of each branch, there was a large piece of red fruit. He told me the fruit at the end of the branch was very good, but that you had to be very careful when you tried to get it—not an untenable description of his relationship with his mother. It may have also signaled his transference to me and explained his initial cautious behavior with me.

In the first month of treatment, he played out a repetitive fantasy, using just the mother and father dolls. The father was portrayed as provocative and wild; the mother was portrayed as an angry, punitive woman, obsessed with having a clean house and having everything in place. Note how Denny identified with both mother and father with regard to this behavior. Denny played out the role of the mother and would instruct me what to do as the father. After setting up the scene with an overly careful attention to detail, he would have the father deliberately provoke the mother into beating him. The father constantly messed up by moving the furniture out of place which would enrage the mother.

In the following hour, there was a slight variation on the theme, and it was about this time that he began to show marked improvement in school. In fact, he actually brought home a good report card. Denny walked into my office with his usual somber expression. He said he wanted to draw, and then he very carefully drew what he said was the outside of his home, taking particular care with the overhang of the roof. He told me of a time when he threw a flying saucer up on the roof and his father put him on the roof to retrieve the saucer—then insisted that he jump down. He told me he was frightened. At this point, he drew a bird's nest on the side of the house. He said that he found one there and took it down. He wanted to look at the baby birds. He thought he would take it to school and show the birds to the kids. The father discovered what he had done and whipped him. I suggested that some kids would feel hurt and angry if their fathers did that; he said that he did get angry with his father and with his mother too.

He put the drawing aside and walked over to the dollhouse. He commented that I must see other children, because the dollhouse was different. He liked to have things just the way he left them. I said I guessed he wished that I didn't see other children. "How many children do you see?" he wanted to know. "What are their names?" I simply answered that, like at home, he seemed to be afraid that I would not have enough time left over for him. He grinned and said yes. The mother at this time was babysitting seven neighborhood children.

Denny then set about putting the furniture in the playhouse. As usual, he was very careful and exacting in the way he did this. While he was doing this, he had me making little balls out of clay which he said were to be spaghetti for dinner. He started out the play as usual by acting out the mother's role. He had the mother doll sweeping out the room, using the paintbrush as the broom. I was to be the father. He instructed me to come into the room and knock the furniture out of place, whereupon he, as the mother, beat the father unmercifully. This was played out several times. I told him that I thought he seemed to want the mother to beat him up. He laughed and he agreed. I asked why this was. He didn't respond. Instead, he said *he* now wanted to be the father. This was the first time this had occurred in his play sessions.

Denny announced that this time he was not going to tell me what to say. I was to be the mother, but Denny made it quite clear that I was on my own.

He was wild as the father. He knocked over the furniture and then the dollhouse. The father became increasingly more powerful. He could then fly. He flew through the roof of the dollhouse. He told me that the house was now on fire. I think he was disgusted with me for just standing by, for he finally took the mother doll out of my hands and proceeded to pummel the father doll. He then called the ambulance for him. I said that I could see that he wanted the mother to stop this wild daddy.

In subsequent hours, he spoke of his many fears—his fears of a car accident on the freeway, his concern about people who rode motorcycles—they might get squashed, his fear of living in a house—didn't I think it was safer to live in an apartment? He advised: "Maybe you should put up a 'Beware of Dog' sign, even if you don't have a dog." He then made a drawing with cutouts, a very picture of a boy taking down baby birds so he could have baby birds of his own. A mother bird was there about to drop a rock on the boy, angry because he had taken her babies. I thought he seemed to be telling me that he was a frightened little boy, frightened of the angry people about him; they had not provided a safe, protected world for him. He would like to care for the baby birds in a way he would like to be protected. But the mother bird was going to physically punish him, as his father actually had. Of course, I also kept in mind his wish to rid the mother of his younger siblings.

One hour he came in and told me how he now had a bird and that he was taming his bird, so that he could carry her about everywhere in the house. "How big will my bird grow?" he asked me. I asked him how big he wanted his bird to grow. He said that he wished that she would grow very big and then she could carry him around. I made an obvious observation: I said that I guessed that he treated the bird the way he wished he could be treated. He agreed, but he went on to make a drawing that perhaps gives us another part of the answer; namely, that he would like to grow up, but that growing up was filled with danger as well as pleasure. He drew a speeding car, a stop sign, and a house in the distance. In the sky he drew a bad guy with a helicopter. He took a great deal of pleasure in jazzing up the car with lights. When I commented that he would probably like to be like his father who speeds about, but added that Denny was worried about what might happen to him if he got out of control; he told me that his father gets a lot of tickets for his speeding, and he also gets into accidents. At this point I have described the first three months of treatment. Denny made remarkable gains during this period.

Denny had two bouts with the flu about this time and missed several sessions with me. When he returned, he appeared very pale and thin. In the following hour he played out the family drama and gave what I would imagine to be very accurate picture of the family scene. This was the first time he used the boy doll in his play and identified with him.

After his usual careful setting up of the scene, the play began. The mother was very efficient, ordering the boy around, annoyed that he had messed up in the bathroom. The boy cleaned up, obviously trying to be good. This probably related to his difficult toilet training period. The father then came home late and the mother was very angry at him for this. The father flew about the room. The boy knocked the mother off the counter which Denny called the cliff, but then he saved her. He told her that she was mean, that she was not his mother, and that his father was not his father. He knocked them both off the cliff again and saved them once more. I said that the boy gets very angry with his father and mother and wishes he could throw them away, but he loves them too and brings them back. I said that I bet he gets very upset when his parents fight. He answered that he did and that sometimes he gets in there and fights too.

The next time I saw him he seemed very annoyed. He told me that he was not going to be able to come for the next two sessions, because he was going to be a ring bearer at a wedding—his aunt's wedding. He went on to tell me that he was pleased about it but he did not know what he had to do. I suggested we could play it out with the dolls. This is the fantasy he enacted with the dolls.

The boy was very worried because he did not know what to do and in short order was expressing his anger at his parents for making him go to the wedding. He gathered up all of the dolls he had placed at the wedding and told me he was going to drown them. In an ingenious way, he wrapped them together with some wire and attached them to the faucet in my office sink, hanging them from their feet while he filled the sink with water. He used large beads to torpedo them under the water.

The boy was very powerful in this play. Denny used straws as stilts that he attached with Scotch tape to the doll's legs to make him taller. At this point, he pulled out the father doll from the rest of the group and proceeded to beat him because he did not know the answer to 2+2. After a good beating, he pronounced the father dead. I said that the boy gets scared when he thinks he cannot do something right and then he tries to act tough like the people he is afraid of. I told him I could see he was scared about being the ring bearer, and maybe we could talk to his parents about exactly what he had to do. Denny seemed very pleased about this. When I mentioned it to his father, however, the father told me he thought it was good for kids to be scared—they learn better under such conditions.

I did not see Denny for about three weeks. He had regressed during this period. He had missed a month of school, during which time his mother was in a car accident and was bedridden. His teacher reported that he had become fearful in school, even unable to hold a pencil to write. He would also have tantrums when confronted with difficult tasks.

In the first session after his return, he seemed sober and tense. He did not even greet me. He sat down and just stared at me. Then he held up his hands to show me his badly picked fingernails. He played out the following fantasy: the boy doll he called David was sleeping in the bedroom. In the kitchen, the mother took hold of the father and kicked him out of the house because he was mean. She did not want him around anymore. When David awakened, he was very powerful. He stood on the table, making himself taller than his mother. Denny made a point of saying the boy doll was taller. David took hold of the mother and tossed her out. Denny told me David did this because his parents were so mean.

I told Denny I would really like to figure out why David is so upset with his parents. I don't usually direct the content of a child's fantasy, but this day I wanted to go over some of the traumatic events that occurred in the last couple months, in order to see what I could learn and hopefully to help Denny integrate and make sense out of what had happened. I said that David had been sick and that he was just beginning to feel better. I brought him out of the bedroom. His mother and father announced to him that he had to be ring bearer at a wedding. Denny immediately took over the role of the boy. "I don't want to be ring bearer," he said; and he kicked the parents across the room. "Why does that make you mad David?" I asked. His answer was that he did not like marriages, that people get mean when they get married; and he staunchly announced: "I never want to get married!"

He then stated that the boy was like Superman, and he could fly. He tied a small diaper around the boy's neck which was to act as Superman's cape. He said that the boy was flying into the desert, and he instructed me to be both parents. I was to walk on the ground and look for him; whereas he would fly.

"Come back, come back!" I cried. "You have to be the ring bearer!" "No!" He responded in a very determined fashion. "No!" He then proceeded to beat up the parents. He took off his Superman cape and tied the parents up with it so that they were immobilized. "They are dead," he proclaimed. "Now we have to bury them." He wanted me to find a coffin for them. I found an appropriate box, and he proceeded to hold a burial ceremony.

"I thought you were going to tell this story," he said to me. I told him I would continue. I took the boy doll and placed him in a chair. I said he was in school now and, speaking for the boy doll, I said that he was very nervous, that he could not even write—in fact, he could not do anything; and he even had a tantrum when the teacher pressured him to work. Denny looked at me suspiciously and said very pointedly, "I can write!" I told him that I knew that, but this boy could not, and I wondered what was troubling him. Denny responded, "He is alone now. His mother and father are dead." He then placed the boy in the house that he had built and knocked down the house in such a way that the blocks covered the boy. I said, "The world seems to be falling down on this boy." He threw more blocks on top of the boy. I then cried out, "David, David! Your parents are not dead. You just wish that they were dead because you are so angry with them."

Denny looked very pleased. "Yeah!" he said, and he took the boy over to the place where the parents were buried. "You are not dead!" he told them, and then untied them. "In fact, you can fly too." He made a point of saying that the boy David was able to fly higher than his parents, but when I said that I guessed that David wanted to be more powerful than his father and mother so he wouldn't have to be afraid of them, Denny gave me a set, determined look. "He doesn't just want to be, he is!" He looked very pleased with himself as he said this.

It was the end of the session, and Denny said something to me he had never said before. In a very sincere sounding voice, he said, "Thank you." We both felt we had had a very good hour together. I learned that he had a very good week in school following this session. What came out so clearly in this hour, as in previous ones, was Denny's horrific dilemma. The people he so desperately needed to care for him, support him, were also felt to be his persecutors.

Denny was able to stay in school the remainder of the year. He had his ups and downs; but, basically, he was able for the first time to perform satisfactorily in school, at least until the end of the school year. Therapy was terminated abruptly when the mother divorced the father, was awarded custody of the children, and moved out of the state. Denny's emotional and behavioral difficulties were his way of coping with traumatic incidents and severe mental and physical abuse: sometimes he would identify with the aggressor; other times he would fall into a severe regressed state. Psychoanalytically oriented psychotherapy provided Denny with the opportunity to understand how his mind worked via a new object, as the two of us explored the underlying meaning of his imaginative play. This helped to lessen his anxiety and aggression, and positively affected his relationships, his adjustment in school, and his ability to learn. Clearly it did not indicate that his problems were due to some form of brain impairment.

Recent national surveys have indicated a marked increase in the ADHD diagnosis. The number of children and adults diagnosed with ADHD rose from 900,000 in 1990 to almost 5 million in 1998. Moreover, there has been an increasing tendency to prescribe stimulant medication for its treatment. According to a report presented to the Drug Enforcement Administration in 1998, prescriptions rose 700 percent since 1990; whereas the number of children receiving psychotherapy for ADHD fell from 40 percent in 1989 to 25 percent in 1996 (Jones, 2002). I imagine it has dropped even lower by now.

Many parents prefer to believe there is a neurological basis for their children's disturbed behavior, as it relieves the guilt that the child's difficulties may be related to their inadequate parenting skills. This tends to mask the family entanglements that might contribute to an overstimulating environment.

Lawrence Diller in his book *Running on Ritalin*, states and I quote: "Ritalin seems to have become the drug for our day. As competition on every level intensifies, our preoccupations as a culture increasingly center on performance. And our children, whether we realize it or not, have been serving as a proving ground for the premise of medicating to enhance performance."

There is also the tendency of some educators and parents as well to use the ADHD label as a means to medicate and subdue an irritating, impulsive child without any attempt to understand the psychological determinants of his behavior. Just as we know that aspirin often can reduce a fever, we know that Ritalin often can reduce troublesome behavior; however, just as it is crucial to understand the underlying causes of the fever and not stop with reducing the symptom, it is crucial to understand the underlying causes of ADHD behavior.

I also agree with Robert Furman when he stated in an unpublished paper: "All the symptoms listed (for ADHD) could result from the behavior of a normally rambunctious child or else could be caused by any of an almost endless list of childhood disturbances. For in truth the list is a list of manifestations of a child in distress, either within himself or with his environment or a combination of both. . . . In point of fact, the ADHD child, rather than having a diagnosis, is a child in need of a study to obtain a diagnosis." I too believe the condition described as ADHD can have many different symptoms and causes; and, I reiterate: in some cases, it may include a neuropsychological abnormality that is best treated with medication. But—a cautionary note: beware the rush to judgment!

In the chapter that follows, the subject of revenge and the guilt it evokes will be explored.

Chapter Eight

Grapes of Wrath

Revenge has often been a central theme in literature (e.g. Dante's *Inferno*, Shakespearean plays (e.g. Hamlet, Dumas' *The Count of Monte Cristo*), in Greek mythology (Sophocles' Oedipus the King), in politics (the Israelis versus the Palestinians, and in religion (God visiting the plague on the Egyptians: Muslims versus Jews versus Christians). The Los Angeles Times newspaper features an article on the front page of the Health Section entitled "You May be Tempted to Get Even, But Think Twice." In contrast, it has been given scant attention in the psychoanalytic literature. Irvin Rosen (2005), in an attempt to understand this, titled his paper "Revenge: The Hate That Does Not Speak Its Name." Robert Lane (2005) attributes this neglect to Freud's categorizing the topic of revenge to the aggressive drive and a manifestation of the death instinct. A panel held at the winter meeting of the American Psychoanalytic Association in 2004 was the first one to take up the subject of revenge in the history of the American (Beattie, 2004). There is even a greater paucity of any reference to revenge in the child literature. That said, there have been analytic papers that have expanded our understanding of the underlying dynamics of revenge.

Otto Fenichel (1928) cited a case of a male patient who directed his internalized mother's very punitive superego toward himself and toward others, as well as towards his mother: he had fantasies of killing her out of revenge. Fenichel recognized that the hostility his patient expressed against his mother was also directly against himself.

Karen Horney (1948) distinguished vengeful patients from those who were only hostile. According to Horney, vengeful patients experienced severe cruelty and authoritarism in early childhood.

Lucy LaFarge (2006) understands the wish for revenge as a response to narcissistic injury. Hilary Beattie (2004, p. 514) adds it can be a defense against shame, loss and/or guilt; moreover, she points out the adaptive aspect of revenge, as in, it turns passivity into activity. Castelnuovo-Tedesco in a paper entitled "Stealing, Revenge, and the Monte Cristo complex" (1974) focuses on the repressed guilt which he postulates is projected and isolated.

Harold Blum article (1997) holds relevance for the clinical cases presented in this paper. He states that when a child's wishes and demands run counter to those of his parents, especially when there is strict discipline and limits, it is "a developmental inevitability for children and parents to hate each other." (p. 362). The hated child now identifies with the parent he hates and thereby identifies with the aggressor.

Abused children characteristically have a wide range of conflicts and emotional disorders as a function of their developmental experiences. This paper, however, examines some of the common elements that characterize their psychodynamics, particularly the incomplete repression of revenge related to repressed underlying guilt. I'm going to present two clinical cases, a girl 9½ with a school phobia, and a 12-year-old girl with suicidal ideation. Their presenting problems differ, but certain psychodynamics are held in common. I focus on those related to a driving wish to seek revenge and the conflict it ignites. I believe the course of their treatment demonstrates the efficacy of psychoanalytically oriented psychotherapy for these children.

The first case, Janie, age 9, was referred because she suffered from a severe school phobia. She was terrified of going to school and, soon after the parents brought her to school, kicking and screaming and pleading with them not to leave her, the school authorities would notify them that she was ill in the nurse's office. She suffered from stomach aches and nausea. The lunch period was a particularly frightening time; she was afraid that she would vomit and that the other children would ridicule her. She was often obsessed with the idea that her friends disliked her and preferred others. She saw her teacher also as having favorites while rejecting her. The fear of going to school first manifested itself when Janie was seven and in the second grade. Although the problem became increasingly severe, the parents only sought help when Janie's teacher strongly recommended it. The parents saw themselves as conscientious and concerned, but they felt that Janie would outgrow these problems. Janie's mother reported that she too had been frightened of going to school as a child.

Janie was one of three children, all girls: a sister 2½ years younger and another 2½ years older. The parents claimed to remember virtually nothing about Janie as an infant. The mother said that she was too preoccupied with taking care of her own mother to remember, for her mother was a very self-centered woman who constantly demanded to be with her. Both parents likened Janie to this grandmother, expressing fear that she would be a replica—someone who constantly complained of aches and pains and other people not caring enough about her.

It slowly emerged that the parents felt guilty about the way they had treated Janie after the birth of their youngest child. Janie, then 2½, had developed a sleep disturbance, remaining awake for two to three house, crying and screaming. They felt that she was tyrannizing them, and they beat her in desperation. The father was particularly enraged with her. Both parents had been physically abused as children.

From ages 2½ to 7 Janie was usually left in the care of the maternal grandmother, as the oldest daughter had developed a severe gastrointestinal disturbance at this time that often required hospitalization. The parents were very preoccupied with this child's illness; they frequently had to take her for visits to the doctor and to the hospital.

The school phobia developed shortly after her grandfather died in an automobile accident. It occurred on Janie's birthday which was on the 13th of the month.

I saw Janie in analytically oriented psychotherapy over a period of three years—the first year, three times weekly, the second year, twice a week, and then on a once a week basis. In my first session with Janie, she appeared as a sweet, frightened little girl, looking younger than her 9½ years. There was an infantile quality about her speech. It was quite apparent that she was eager to please me and seemed rather stiff and inhibited, as if fearful I might be critical of her. She readily told me she was afraid of going to school and especially eating in school, lest she vomit. She said that she had had this problem since the second grade when she saw a yard teacher with a brace on his back, looking as if he had been in an accident. It made her feel queasy and gave her a stomach ache.

In her fantasy play, Janie was a different child; she was spontaneous, enthusiastic, creative, and very dramatic. Her settings were always very elaborate with great attention to detail. For her first fantasy, she used the building blocks to set up two residences side by side. In one lived the A. family (she used her own surname) and in the other, Mrs. Fine. "Not you, of course," she assured me. Mr. A. was very troubled by his children. He wanted his wife all for himself, and he was very distressed by the fighting in the home. The mother wanted more children, but the father was opposed to it. He felt that the family was large enough. The father was obviously echoing Janie's sentiments. The little girl in the family had nightmares, but she cautioned the parents not to go to Mrs. Fine for help because Mrs. Fine was a witch—"Not you, of course," again she assured me.

Janie de-powered me by changing the story-line. In this way she was able to distance herself from the idea she was describing her concerns to a cruel omnipotent woman, (a negative mother transference?). Her fantasy revolved around two girls, Wendy and Lisa, next-door neighbors and best friends, each with a baby in their own family. Janie gave herself the role of Wendy, instigator, manipulative, devious, and quite mischievous. I was relegated to the role of Lisa, her tag-along, easily dominated friend. The two girls tormented their parents and the babies. They put insects in their parents' bed and they frightened the babies, first with a spider and then an alligator. Finally they decided to run away, leaving a note for their parents which read, "You don't love me; you love the babies." When Wendy decided to return home, her parents told her that she seemed like a stranger. Janie explained to me that was because Wendy was now a witch, and Wendy would instruct Lisa in the art of witchcraft. The parents were to be kept ignorant of Wendy and Lisa's magical power, while Wendy and Lisa were all knowing about what the parents were doing, because they had placed invisible tape recorders in every room. In order to maintain their status as witches, they had to eat rotten food—raw hot dogs and raw eggs.

In my interpretations, which were offered by Lisa, I tried to put her in touch with her rage and her destructive wished toward the baby who usurped her place. In fact, by using listening devices, it would seem that she hoped to top her parents from even making babies in the first place. I thought it a charming bit of symbolism to use raw hot dogs and eggs for the supreme creative act. The underlying wish was to have the mother all to herself. I told her that I thought she began to feel herself to be a witch when she felt so mean toward the babies, and maybe she did not want the parents to find out, because they might not want her around if they knew. She vehemently disagreed with my last suggestion, "No," she insisted, "she did not want the parents to find out because they would take away her power." I stressed that she wanted to hold onto the idea that she could be very powerful; it gave her hope that she could find some way to make things better for herself. Meantime, Janie improved remarkably. The school phobia seemed to have vanished for the time being, and she even began to eat lunch in school. Why the sudden improvement? Perhaps it helped to vent her vengeful fantasies and this temporarily empowered her. And perhaps my acceptance of these fantasies without her having to fear retribution helped to reduce her anxiety. This in turn may have promoted a positive transference and a temporary flight into health.

Janie informed me that she now wanted to change the story. Lisa and Wendy were no longer witches. Now they did not have any parents, because the parents did not want them anymore; the parents preferred to travel. While they were traveling, Wendy had a birthday party and one of her birthday wishes was that her parent would come back changed, that they would not be suspicious of her anymore. I suggested that it might be the other way around, too—that maybe she wished she did not have to be suspicious of them and worry about whether they loved her or not, for that was what made her so angry with them and stirred up her wish to get rid of them.

The relatively symptom-free period lasted a few months; but approximately a month before her birthday, Janie once again became extremely fearful of going to school. The fear seemed to be triggered by her reaction to an argument she had had with her mother. One of Janie's friends had wanted her to wear a certain dress to school, and the mother opposed this. At first, Janie tried to be defiant, but as the mother became increasingly upset and hysterical, Janie complained of being dizzy and refused to go to school. It was shortly after this that Janie tried to prove to me that wishing can make it so, giving me examples of times when her wished did come true. She also expressed her concern that this year her birthday was going to fall on Friday the 13th. Friday became the most dreaded day of the week, and the day she most feared going to school.

She became obsessed with the idea that she might be kidnapped on the way to school. She stopped eating lunch, and there were terrible scenes at home in the morning when she resisted going to school. As Janie regressed, the mother became increasingly explosive and threatening. It was characteristic of the mother to say, "You're killing me," and even to demonstrate by holding a knife to her throat. It was at this point that I referred the mother for treatment.

The fantasy material changed during this disturbed period. Janie tome me that Wendy did not want her friend Lisa to butt into her business right now. In other words, I was to keep quiet and not offer any interpretations. A snow monster came to Wendy's family, and the family was very frightened. The snow monster attacked the house, beating on it and making growling and biting noises. The baby was particularly in danger. The father armed himself with a rifle. I said that I thought I understood why she did not want Lisa around. Janie laughed and responded, "Yes, because her mother would turn on her and get angry and divorce her." She was able to bring out how upsetting it was to her that her own mother would encourage her to express her anger, then contradict herself by falling apart. Indeed, the mother experienced Janie's angry feelings as a kind of murderous attack. I suggested that she was sometimes afraid to express such feeling to me because I might react like her mother.

The fantasy play continued. The father had to go on a trip. He took Wendy's pet crocodile with him and it began to snap at him and bite him. This compounded the father's problems because he was also worried that somebody might steal his gold, and it was stolen. The father became ill and ran a high temperature, on the day Wendy's birthday party was planned. Around this time, Janie developed a fear that her father would have a heart attack and began to carefully monitor what he ate. I felt this play indicated how angry Janie was that her father got into financial difficulty and how fearful she was that her angry thoughts would harm her father.

As we explored these feelings, Janie recalled that her grandfather's automobile accident occurred on her birthday. She had been angry with him because he had left her party early and characteristically she felt this was a sign of neglect. She, therefore, came to feel that in some way she was instrumental in his dying, because she had been angry with him. She thought that her birthday was unlucky, and she was afraid that she might die or that something might happen to her mother or father on her birthday. In the fantasy play, Janie had Wendy's grandmother die of a heart attack, and Wendy became very angry with herself because she felt that it was her fault.

As a result of playing out this material in fantasy Janie was able to express how disturbed she was after her grandfather's death. It was as if her grandmother had died also, because her mother had prohibited the grandmother from visiting her at this time. Janie felt responsible for the grandmother's banishment as well. In an elaborate fantasy, Janie offered an explanation for such feelings: Wendy's parents left her for a few months with a married couple whom they hired to babysit. She grew to love them and wished they were her parents. When her parents returned, she treatment them as if they were strangers, admittedly out of rage because they had left her.

The babysitters wanted to adopt her, and a court battle followed with all the trimmings of a jury trial. It was impressive the way she set up the courtroom. Witnesses were placed on the stand to testify that her parents had neglected her. She felt so guilty about breaking up the friendship between the parents and the babysitters that she pretended to be ill and, claimed she was unable to appear in court, where she was supposed to decide with whom she wanted to live. The judge was forced to make a decision for her, and he placed her in the custody of the babysitters. The mother secretly admitted to the judge that she hated Wendy because Wendy liked the babysitters better and, moreover, the mother knew that Wendy hated her.

Although Wendy was very happy with her new parents, she soon developed stomach aches and feared eating lunch in school, particularly at those times when other children in the classroom got more attention. It was an easy connection for Janie and for me to relate her fantasy play to that time when her grandparents were here babysitters. She told me that in anger she would sometimes tell her mother that she wished her grandparents were her real parents, and she would daydream about running away and finding more loving parents. I suggested that she must have felt very sad and lonely and left out at that time. Yes, she told me, like Oliver Twist. She explained that Oliver Twist was supposed to ask for more food because he drew the shortest straw; but when he did, they became very angry with him and put him up for sale. I thought that Janie was terrified that her neediness and demanding behavior might lead to her abandonment.

It appeared that the fantasies that Janie played out in her sessions with me captured her view of her life experiences, bringing to light her anger and feelings of rejection when her parents left her with the babysitting grandparents, as well as her rage when her mother denied the grandmother visitation. When her hatred and death wishes toward her mother linked up with her belief in her magical powers, it made separating from the mother and going to school a terrifying experience. The fantasies of running away and finding new parents became a nightmare to her after her grandfather's death and the absence of the grandmother. I repeatedly interpreted her belief in her magical power to destroy others, not only as an expression of rage, but as a desperate need to feel she had some control over her destiny. The end of the babysitter episode in the Wendy's saga heralded the end of Janie's school phobia. The opportunity to play out revenge fantasies in therapy where their hidden meaning was interpreted helped Janie distinguish fantasy from reality and lowered her anxiety level as well as her rage.

The content of her play began to contain oedipal themes—fantasies in which Wendy competed with other girls for the love of a popular fellow. The only residue of her separation anxiety was contained in her reluctance to spend the night at a friend's house. Janie had wanted to work this one last problem out, and there was some indication that she wanted to hold onto the problem in order to continue our relationship. The father had another business failure, they moved, and treatment had to be terminated. A month later, Janie had a set-back with a short-lived return of her presenting symptoms: fear of going to school and fear of eating in school. The anxiety subsided after she spoke to me briefly on the telephone and related her fears to the fact her mother was so upset about the family's financial crisis. Janie maintained a telephone contact with me for a couple years and basically retained her gains in therapy.

The second case to be described is that of a 12-year-old girl to be called Annie. She was referred when she expressed some suicidal ideas. She was seen in psychotherapy twice weekly for approximately 2½ years. Annie was a pretty girl, feminine and fragile in appearance, with small, delicate features. In the early months of treatment, she usually wore a very forlorn, worried expression. She was overly polite in her manner and excessively concerned about pleasing me. She was obsessed with that idea that her father would die. At times, she would be overwhelmed with anxiety, as she imagined him having a heart attack or an automobile accident. Other times, she feared that she would be stabbed and slept with her arm in a special way to protect herself and to ward off attack. She confided that she thought she was chosen by God to have special powers and special knowledge. She occasionally heard a voice—her voice—that had the power to grant all her wishes. There were times when she would climb into a storage cabinet above her closet in her bedroom. Here she had her omnipotent fantasies. Here, reality did not exist for her.

Her mother claimed that she had no idea Annie had any problems until she made her suicidal threat. Annie was her second child in a family of four children—three girls, and the youngest child, the long awaited boy. The mother appeared as a rather tense person, eager to be viewed as a "good woman." She stressed that she and Annie were very much alike, that while her husband expressed his feelings readily, she tended to hide them, especially her anger. She viewed Annie as very fragile and felt most protective toward her. Annie was the most feminine of her daughters. Her youngest daughter, on the other hand, was a tomboy and had spoken openly for her wish to be a boy and marry a woman. The mother felt very guilty about this, because she felt it related to the fact that she and her husband had very much wanted a son.

The father, who refused to meet with me, was described as a patriarch who expected his wife and children to cater to him. He was given to emotional outbursts. On a couple of occasions, he had damaged or broken through a wall with his fist when he became enraged. When the children were small, he would beat them with a special riding crop, which he had bought for the expressed purpose. His theory was that it was only necessary to beat the children when they were young, as that instilled fear in them and conditioned them to be good later. The father encouraged magical thinking. He told Annie that it was dangerous to be envious. When he was in the Air Corps, he envied his friend who had a better plane than he did and his friend's plane crashed.

Early in the treatment, I pointed out to Annie that like her father, she too seemed to think thoughts were very powerful. She readily confirmed this and told me how disturbing it was to have thoughts about her father dying, for she feared the thoughts themselves would bring about his death. She had erected a poorly functioning obsessional structure in an attempt to control the rage within her that so terrified her. This was reflected in a therapy hour in the third month of treatment.

In this hour she told me about her voice and its ability to grant wishes. I said that I guessed she would like to think that some powerful being could magically make her wishes come true. She agreed, and then told me she had thoughts that she could not stop and wished she could. For example, she would repeatedly see the rings of a loose-leaf notebook and imagine she could take them out. She also imagined that she had a packet of thoughts in her wrist. She would then remove them with a key, put them in her head, then take out another packet of thoughts to place back in her wrist. She feared that I would think her thoughts were silly. I told her that I was glad she was able to tell me about them because I was able to understand her better. It meant to me that she would like to remove her disturbing thoughts. She told me that he indeed had thoughts that she would like to remove. Recently, she had been afraid that her little brother, age 6, would die. In some clumsy way, he would hurt himself and himself. I drew out her feelings about him, and she elaborated how he annoyed her, how ashamed she felt about him.

I told her that I knew of a girl who also had a kid brother, and sometimes she would get so angry with him that she wished he were not around anymore. But then she would become frightened, because she loved her brother too and was afraid her wish would come true. With great feeling, Annie said, "That sums up the way I feel about Jimmie. I'm afraid to think such things. I'll put a curse on him and make it happen." As if to offer proof, she told me she was able to wish herself sick; but when I asked her how, she half-smiled as she told me she could get a cold in a draft. It gave me opportunity to point out to her that to make a wish come true, she really had to do something to make it happen. She confessed that sometimes she had a fantasy in which she would take a kitchen knife and plunge it into Jimmie, but she really did not think she would.

Her magical thinking was not easily dismissed despite the apparent acceptance of my first interpretation about it. When I suggested links between her hate and anger toward her father, which she had begun to express, and her fear that he would die, she became extremely disturbed. At the same time, when I attempted to differentiate between thought and act to indicate that she was not, in fact, all powerful but with only human sized anger, she was furious with me. She accused me of de-powering her and said that she refused to let my de-powering words have any effect on her because she was special. She preferred her closet to seeing me, for there she was all powerful in league with God. He had confided in her, but insisted she must not talk to anyone else. He had chosen her because she was special and had conferred upon her special powers to know the secrets of life and death and the creation of the world. Annie reminded me of an important dictate in therapeutic technique: one must have a healthy respect for a patient's need to maintain his or her defensive structure. Annie was right. I believe that I pusher her too hard at this time.

For a period of time Annie became more distant and more sullen. Then she hit upon the idea of proving to herself and to me that she was indeed endowed with special powers. Her plan revolved around the following situation: Annie had been very close to a young aunt who had since married in Israel and recently had a baby. Annie freely expressed how angry and disappointed she was that her aunt had a child and that she no longer had her special relationship with her. I suspected that she transferred the earlier rage that she had felt toward her own mother for having babies on to this safer person; however, she felt that she hurt her mother by feeling this way. She tried to remedy her hostile thoughts by buying a certificate for a tree to be planted in Israel in honor of her aunt's new baby. The certificate was to be sent to her mother, and it was to be a surprise.

Annie had a dream in which the certificate arrived and when her mother examined it, she scoffed. Annie wept inconsolably in the dream; she was so hurt that her mother would react this way. She told me how happy she would really be, if her mother would actually scoff when she received the certificate. Although it would mean that the mother knew it was an empty gesture, it would confirm the predictive value of her dream. I reminded her how badly she had felt after she had told her mother that she did not like her aunt anymore. "Yes," she said, "I wanted my mother to be very touched by what I had done, spending all my money for the certificate." I interpreted, "It would be very painful for you to think your mother might see through you and I believe that is why you cried so hard in your dream, but you've turned it around to make it a nice a happening. You tried to get rid of the pain by believing your dream predict the future." Annie accepted my interpretation and put it to use. She told her mother about her gift to her aunt: fortunately the mother did not scoff.

Two interrelated themes developed: one involved a compelling wish to maintain a symbiotic tie to her mother and the other, an uncontrollable need to torment her younger sister by teasing her. She spoke of wanting to tune in very carefully to what her mother wanted of her. She had the fantasy of being inside her mother's head, so that she would know exactly how she felt. This wish was also reflected in her relationship to her hallucinatory voice that she believed was tuned into all her needs and wishes.

Her friendships had broken up, because her friends never became as tuned into her needs as she wanted them to be. She did not want to have to tell them what she wanted. She felt that they should sense it intuitively. As we explored this powerful need for symbiotic bonding, she revealed how overly sensitive she was to her mother's hurt feelings and recognized that such feelings were intensified when she acted independently of the mother. To become an individual in her own right, to grow up, meant the death of that special symbiotic relationship with her mother.

The dynamic was exemplified in one particular session. In this hour, she told how she had to learn the Torah for her Bas Mitzvah and so far she had only learned part of it. The night before, her mother had asked her to recite it and questioned why she had not yet learned all of it. That night she had a dream in which her mother appeared mean and demanding and forced her to recite the Torah at her Bas Mitzvah, even though she was not ready to do so. She then spoke of her fear of growing up, her wish to remain a child, her anger with her mother when she pushed her to assume more responsibility, how she hated the idea of growing older and of dying. She added that she was preoccupied with thoughts of her mother's death and hers as well. Over and over again, she would close her eyes and imagine herself dying. I suggested that the death she was mourning was that of the little child in her—a little child who wanted to be so close to her mother that they would almost be one. She saw her younger sister as a threat to the close tie she wanted to her mother, and she teased her unmercifully with her biting, sarcastic remarks.

The insights and self-awareness Annie derived from our work together seemed to promote her psychic growth. More and more she filled the sessions with her sibling rivalrous feelings. Her mood fluctuated markedly depending on whether she felt others, particularly her parents and her teachers, thought her special and accepted her. However, there were fewer and fewer references to her magical thinking, and the anxieties relating to death fears and wishes disappeared. She seemed to be turning more to people than to her fantasy world of omnipotence and omniscience to gratify her strong narcissistic needs.

A few months later, she attempted to reinstate her magical thinking by entertaining the idea she ad ESP powers. She had learned that I had children, and it was very upsetting to her. She became cold and distant and even threatened to stop treatment. She asked why I bothers to call my patients by name. Why didn't I just give them numbers? They did not really mean anything to me. One day she came into my office appearing quite cheerful. She was so pleased to tell me that through her ESP, she learned that I had a 15 year old son of whom I was very fond and very proud. Surprisingly, she accepted my interpretation that it was a comforting thought to think she had ESP powers; it protected her against the pain of feeling I preferred boys to her, like she felt her parents did.

I continued to see Annie for approximately another year. The period that has been reviewed covered about a year and a half treatment. Her anxieties, particularly as they expressed themselves in her phobias, diminished considerably. She began to function exceedingly well in school. Whereas before she had shown considerable promise, she had been unable to concentrate in school, because she was so absorbed in her daydreaming and with her anxieties. She graduated from junior high school valedictorian of her class. Her social relationships with other youngsters and with teachers also markedly improved. In her remaining sessions, she dealt primarily with her intense feelings of sibling rivalry and her over dependence on her mother.

Shortly after we had set a termination date, Annie brought me the following dream: she felt somehow compelled to enter a house where she knew there were monsters. It was dark in there and frightening. The monsters appeared like grizzly bears. She feared for her life, but as her eyes grew more accustomed to the dark, and she could see them more clearly, they were not threatening at all; in fact, they appeared rather friendly. As she looked into a corner, she saw someone like the Wizard of Oz. He had been making the bears behave as if they were monsters. She came to like them and was saddened at the thought of having to leave them when it was time to go. On her way out of the house, she met a girl named Sarah. Somehow she knew that they would be life-long friends. Together they walked back into the daylight and to reality. Annie then told me that her middle name was Sarah. She had hated the name and did not want anyone to know what it was. I thought that the dream signified that Annie's monsters were of her own making, and once she was able to understand this, she could more easily accept rejected parts of herself. I also thought that the dream suggested that she was ready to terminate.

Discussion

The two cases I presented differed in their age, presenting problems and symptoms, but they shared an underlying dynamic related to their wish for revenge. Janie developed a severe school phobia to protect her and her parents from her rage towards them. In her fantasy she plotted revenge against her parents and her grandfather. Annie used grandiose thinking to blanket her death wishes towards her family members, only to have that tactic backfire and lead to suicidal ideation because of the enormity of her guilt and her belief in the power of her magical thinking. Each child experienced a tripartite sequence: 1) they felt weak, anxious, fearful of an external object; 2) they identified with the aggressor—becoming vengeful, unruly, disruptive, entertaining death wishes; and mastery versus helplessness and ungovernable anxious fury (Blum, 1979). These children were cruelly beaten by their parents. When they felt they were the abusers, they no longer experienced themselves as victims. They became the jurors/judges/persecutors. The unfortunate downside was the guilty knowledge of their own evil which produced a school phobia, learning problems, general fearfulness, and eating disorder and/or suicidal ideation.

Jane Goldberg (2006), on the other hand, has an opposite view of revenge fantasies. She writes that "Vengefulness maintains the balance of the destructive drive by directing it away from the self. It is self-protective and stabilizing to the psyche." My clinical experience refutes such a conclusion, but maybe her view may only apply to those who have not experienced brutality in their early childhood. Beattie agrees that "There is a positive adaptation that involves turning passivity into activity," but she adds "that it can be very maladaptive," as evidenced by the three cases she presents.

It has been brought to my attention it seemed remarkable that the patients I described improved rapidly as they did, given the fact that their presenting problems were as severe as they were. I believe that my attempt to understand how they felt and why, was such a contrast to how those who peopled they world treated them that I became the accepting parental figure they longed to have. I could help them understand why they sought vengeance and its unfortunate consequences in the form of hostile, phobic and/or suicidal ideation. These children came to understand that their anger frightened them. Also they may have realized that their parents won't retaliate. After all, the parents brought them to see me. Not only were they rid of their omnipotent fantasies but in addition they were not returning to their original relationship with their parents. All the parents, with the exception of Annie's father, gained from the parent consultations.

I acknowledge that there is some question as to how psychotherapy helps children (Barish, 2004). To quote Kenneth Barish ". . . how a child makes use of interpretation is problematic" (p. 285). He stresses the importance of the relationship, especially the "holding" function. I certainly agree that the nature of the therapeutic relationship is crucial; however, it is my experience that psychoanalytically oriented psychotherapy provides children with an opportunity to understand how their mind works via a new person, who is supportive of their growth and one able to convert (by interpretation) their unsettling fantasies, and their resultant fears, into sensible human understandings of what was happening in their lives. It clearly provided Janie and Annie with a newfound ability to test reality, which in turn helped to soften their punitive superegos, the heirs of parental introjects. They now more easily distinguished reality from fantasy. Although their reality was far from benign, they realized that their frightening monsters, born out of a wish for revenge, were of their own making, no more powerful than the Wizard of Oz.

In the next chapter the psychodynamics of the abused child and the abusive parent will be examined.

Chapter Nine

The Psychodynamics of Physical and Sexual Child Abuse

The effect on children of torture, hatred, seduction, and rape is a most devastating one in producing developmental arrest. Clearly what ensures survival during the vulnerable period of infancy, when the mind and a separate identity are just beginning to form, is the care of a mothering figure. No one in a mental health profession questions that early good parenting is a basic necessity for healthy psychological development, but what is good parenting? In our Western civilization, there is considerable stress on the need to control the child's impulsive behavior. (As the child's spontaneous phrase "Spare the rod and spoil the child" has been a basic tenet in our society.) There is considerable stress on the need to control a child's impulsive behavior. As the child's spontaneous behavior becomes more and more unpredictable, some parents find it necessary to punish him, not only as a release for their own emotional tension, but because they may be convinced that physical punishment is the best form of child rearing. The warning, "Spare the rod and spoil the child" is a basic tenet in our society. I believe that this emphasis in our culture on controlling the child's impulsive behavior has led to an overdiagnosis of ADHD and a rush to medicate children who are considered unruly.

In this chapter a portrait of those involved in the child abuse syndrome will be presented: the physically abused child, the physically abusive parent, the sexually abused child, and the sexually abusive parent. The psychodynamics of the parent as well as the child will be examined. The case examples in chapters 4, 7, and 8 were all accounts of physically abused children. Another abused patient of mine I will call Susan was also brutally beaten at the ages of one and a half to two and a half, because she was unable to fall asleep; instead she would cry and demand her parents' attention. Her mother in particular was unable to tolerate these demands, and beat her brutally. Susan was an adopted child. She was referred for treatment by the school when she was nine years of age, because she had been physically attacking other children in the school. One time she had used a weapon—a knife. The school suspended her from school and threatened expulsion unless she went into treatment. Susan had made a strong tomboy identification. She walked and talked in an exaggeratedly masculine way. It seemed to give her a great sense of power. She had been known to be verbally abusive to her teachers and, on one occasion, struck one. Her fantasies, however, were rich with a central theme that somewhere her real mother existed and would love her, treat her tenderly, and rescue her one day. This case is an example of the underlying longing these abused children have to be nurtured and treated lovingly.

The clinical cases I have described in this and previous chapters contain certain common denominators. All of the children had been physically abused in their earliest years. All had parents who had been abused as children. In their presenting symptoms, they all manifested severe problems in their school adjustment. Interestingly enough, their presenting symptoms related to marked difficulties in containing their own aggressive impulses. They identified with the aggressor and treated those who peopled their world, either in fantasy or in reality, the way they had been treated early in their life. I noted also that these children all engaged in magical thinking, nothing unusual for latency and pre-latency children; however, it seemed exaggerated in their cases. In a sense, all these children were attempting to master the problems related to their early physical abuse. Their pervasive use of magical thinking, or omnipotent thinking, can be considered a defensive maneuver to stave off their sense of helplessness and insignificance by creating an aura about themselves as special and all-powerful. Where this type of thinking becomes linked with destructive thoughts and feelings, it can create new monsters in the form of phobias, learning problems, and a multitude of interpersonal difficulties involving aggression, separation, and invitation. The provocative defiance some of these children displayed with teachers, parents, and peers could definitely be considered a form of mastery. They were irrationally beaten by their parents. When they can make it happen, they have some control.

Sylvia Brody has done extensive research in mother-child interaction. She proposes that the tendency to hit or spank a child is deeply rooted in a defense against the fantasy of being beaten; and the act itself is both a loss of ego organization at the same time that there is an almost frantic attempt to reassert control. There is a wild effort to direct the child's aggression back onto the child.

What seems to be basic in the abuser's attitude toward infants is a conviction that children exist in order to satisfy parental needs. These parents very often feel unloved and look forward to having a baby because that baby will love them. Should the baby be uncooperative and make parental caretaking difficult, the parent may feel disapproved of and unloved and respond with physical abuse as a justifiable reaction to the provocation. Very often the abusive parent tends to see his child as a replica of himself as a bad child. I became very clear in my work with Denny's father that he viewed Denny, in a sense, as the bad part of himself, and had to punish his child the way his father had punished him.

There is a very strong narcissistic wound in these parents. They are exquisitely sensitive to any hint of lack of love or approval and to rejection of any kind. When these feelings of disapproval or rejection are aroused, it becomes a very important factor in triggering individual abusive acts.

It should be emphasized that abusive parents have a wide range of conflicts and character disorders as a function of the variations of their own developmental experience. These factors can be significant in determining which child is more likely to be attacked, when he is attacked, and for what purpose; and they interact closely with the developmental stages of the child. Rigidly obsessive compulsive individuals are more likely to attack their infants when they mess with their food, slobber, or vomit, and later are messy with regard to their excretory functions. In a later phase, such individuals will react when children leave their toys and clothes about. In order that the parent maintain his own repression, he will aggressively attack the child who is stimulating his underlying conflict. If the parent has not resolved his sibling rivalry, this can be a contributing factor to his need to abuse his child. The conflict is likely to related to the need to be loved and nurtured and the feeling that one is not.

A study was conducted by Richard Livingston to determine the difference in psychopathology between physically abused children and sexually abused children. Physically abused children were found to have a much higher incidence of conduct disorder. They repeatedly violated the rights of others, whereas the sexually abused children were found to have more psychotic symptoms (e.g., hallucinations, specifically of a persecutory nature, and severe neurotic symptoms that included depression and feelings of rejection).

Let us now consider some of the developmental issues involved when a child has been physically abused early in life. The major problem begins at a time when the "I" and the "non-I" begin to separate. This occurs around three months of age. Brandt F. Steele, who did extensive research in this area, paraphrased a typical parent in his study: "When I fed Timmy his first solid food at three weeks, he got a hold of the spoon messed the food around. I slapped his hand. He never reached for that spoon again." Steele pointed out that this response indicated that the infant experienced some kind of intrapsychic change concerned with early superego formation, because it demonstrated control and suppression in the infant. The same suppressive child-rearing patterns are likely to be used in subsequent stages of the infant's development. Toilet training may be begun as early as the fourth or sixth month of age and accompanied by criticism, depreciation, and physical abuse, with high expectations for the child to develop other skills as well, such as crawling, walking, talking. Clearly, such parents encourage a very early formation of a punitive superego; at the same time they arouse intensive aggressive, hostile feelings in the child with which the child now has to deal. The child growing up under these circumstances can hardly have a normal oedipal phase, as this stage necessarily is hampered by the already pre-oedipal conflicts and fixations. A little boy with unmet oral needs is too fearful of his mother's rejection or attack to form the appropriate oedipal ties. By the same token, the little girl can only turn to the father with an excessive need for him to supply the basic mothering she has lacked.

In adolescence there is a tendency for the child to experience a restriction on his abilities to explore, observe, and think for himself. Moreover, the child's hostility is provoked when he is physically abused and at the same time he is forbidden to express his hostility overtly, producing an inner conflict of massive proportions and implications. In sum, the victim of brutal physical abuse is robbed of his identity and the ability to maintain authentic feelings. The effects of abuse persist through adulthood. A study conducted with 1,254 college students found that abuse in childhood has enduring affects in adulthood (Burns, Fischer, Jackson, and Harding, 2012).

Now let us examine the psychodynamics of the physically abusive parent. Leonard Shengold has borrowed the term soul murder to designate the cruel and bizarre child-rearing practices involving the physical abuse of children. How can we understand individuals who would inflict such brutality upon their children? The literature is replete with the finding that child abusers were abused as children. Justin Call (1984) has suggested that parents who abuse their children are motivated by what the parents find unacceptable in themselves. The question can be raised, however, as to how do these parents, these battering parents, differ from the disciplinarian who simply views punishment as the best way to achieve the aims of child rearing? A general finding is that such parents are extremely labile in their responses. They have a very low frustration tolerance, so that any tension in their psychic apparatus tends to throw their tenuous emotional stability off balance. This is soon followed by a release of their hostile aggression. As they direct this aggression toward their own child, they often enact actively what they experienced passively as children: They can now identify with the aggressor. If the parent is not latently psychotic, he or she may behave normally between these battering attacks, and may even try to make up to the child for what he or she has done.

A special clinical condition, sometimes referred to as murderous obsessions, can be a derivative of post-partum depression. There are many women who become depressed after childbirth. In very severe post-partum depression, there is sometimes the danger of infanticide.

What seems to be basic in the abuser's attitude toward infants is a conviction that children exist in order to satisfy parental needs. Moreover, these parents very often feel unloved and look forward to having a baby because that baby will love them. Should the baby be uncooperative and make parental care taking difficult, the parent may feel disapproved of and unloved and respond with physical abuse as a justifiable reaction to the provocation. Very often, the abusive parent tends to see his child as a replica of himself as a bad child, as in the case of Denny's father. There is a very strong narcissistic wound in these parents. They are exquisitely sensitive to any hint of lack of love or approval and to rejection of any kind. When these feelings of disapproval or rejection are aroused, it becomes a very important factor in triggering individual abusive acts.

It should be emphasized that abusive parents have a wide range of conflicts and character disorders as a function of the variations of their own developmental experience. These factors can be significant in determining which child is more likely to be attacked, when he is attacked, and for what purpose; and they interact closely with the developmental stages of the child. Rigidly obsessive-compulsive characters are more likely to attack their infants when they mess with their food, slobber, or vomit, and later are messy with regard to their excretory functions. In a later phase, such individuals will react when children leave their toys and clothes about. In order that the parent maintain his own repression, he will aggressively attack the child who is stimulating his underlying conflict.

If a parent has not resolved his sibling rivalry, this can be a contributing factor to his need to abuse his child. The conflict is likely to relate to the need to be loved and nurtured and the feeling that one is not.

While my focus in this chapter has been on the physically abused child, it is not uncommon to find both sexual and physical abuse within a given family. It is also important to keep in mind that some forms of abuse are subtle and elude legal definitions. Although repeatedly allowing the child to witness the primal scene is not considered an illegal act, it can have profoundly disturbing effects on the developing child. In chapter 5 the case of Jonas provides an excellent example. Jonas repeatedly witnessed his parents in the sexual act, and it was an underlying cause of his enuresis.

The following account is an example from one of Jonas's therapy sessions that was not included in the previous chapter. In this session he played out a fantasy in which he was a baby repeatedly beaten by his mother and who purposely made his mother think he wet his bed. The mother in this story sought counseling from Esther. During the consultation, speaking for the mother, he told Esther that the baby wet his bed and I, in the role of Esther, informed the mother that the baby did this, not only because he was so young but because he was very angry with her. Suddenly, two policemen broke into the room and arrested the mother for child abuse. A trial followed. It was held in Germany. Now in the role of the father, Jonas testified that the mother beat the child and named the number of lashes he received. Acting as the judge, I questioned the father as to why the mother did this. He responded that the baby wet and shit in his bed. He then made a point of the fact that he had been wetting for a year and a half, but the mother had been beating him for two years. I, as the judge, drew the obvious conclusion; that is, that the child wet his bed because of the mother's cruelty. American soldiers broke into the courtroom and announced that the mother was wanted for child abuse in the United States, took her back to America, and shot and killed her. The fantasy revealed the rage and powerful wish to retaliate for his mother's cruelty, although he appears to have transferred some of the well-founded anger toward his father onto his mother.

A very interesting research finding is that there is a higher incidence of multiple personality disorder in children who have been abused than is found in the overall statistics relating to the multiple personality disorders. Bowman and his associates suggest that dissociation, the predominant mechanism used in multiple personalities, provides an effective way to cope with the strong affects that are evoked by abuse. This would apply not only to children who are physically abused, but also to the children who have been sexually abused. Wilbur, another researcher of the multiple personality syndrome, suggested that a state of rage is produced in the child when he is abused; and when the child is told that the rage is unacceptable, this in turn leads to the emergence of an alternate personality.

As my review of abused children treated with psychoanalytic psychotherapy strongly suggests, these children and their parents can be helped. It is crucial, of course, that the parents are involved in the treatment.

The tenth and last chapter reviews some of the current psychoanalytic theories.

Chapter Ten

A New Age in Psychoanalysis

Therapeutic action is a term that has been introduced into the psychoanalytic lexicon. It refers to the mechanisms that lead to effective psychoanalytic treatment. Those who have different analytic views of the outcome of analytic treatment have shared their views, often criticizing other perspectives. Earlier chapters in this book have described the Classical, Kleinian and Kernbergian views of psychoanalytic theory and practice, but many others have emerged: intersubjectivity, the Lacanian approach, Renik's view and undoubtedly many more. While it may be apparent that Classical psychoanalytic theory tends to guide my therapeutic work, I have also proposed that it would be ideal if the different analytic theories could all be integrated into one overarching one.

Before undertaking to describe the various views of therapeutic action, I want to examine the concept of the corrective emotional experience and its effect on treatment outcome. It is relevant to the subject of therapeutic action, which focuses on the effectiveness of psychoanalytic therapy and more specifically on the relationship of the analyst with the patient. Several of the current psychoanalytic theories emphasize that it is important for the analyst to be warm and empathic in his relationship with the patient.

The term corrective emotional experience was introduced by Franz Alexander. It referred to the therapist assuming a role to resolve problems related to poor parenting in childhood, for example an overly stern father would be replaced by a gentle, compassionate analyst. According to this definition, an essential ingredient relates to the role playing on the part of the analyst, but one could just as easily define corrective emotional experience as involving any therapeutic process that effects change through some affective interaction with the analyst. In the broader sense, one could then say that any therapeutic effect would necessarily involve a corrective emotional experience. In the first definition, the emphasis is on purposeful role-playing. In the latter, the stress is on the corrective effect of the analyst-patient relationship as a by-product of the therapeutic relationship. However, one could argue that the accepting, affirming attitude of the therapist is also a purposeful technique in effecting change in the patient—a position taken by some of the theorists of therapeutic action. For some, the term has taken on a pejorative meaning. This attitude is primarily held by those analysts who believe that the classical analysis is compromised by a "corrective emotional experience" for it implies that certain parameters have been introduced into the therapeutic process which violate the rule of neutrality on the part of the analyst. Ralph Greenson, however, who would be classified as a classical psychoanalyst, was known to have taken a troubled patient into his home to provide a family experience that he or she had been denied.

Harold Blum, who reflects the Classical perspective, considers the corrective emotional experience a reflection of the analyst's effort to gratify or supply the patient with what was missing in his development, and Blum claims that such an approach tends to sidestep the importance of analyzing archaic conflicts, defenses, and ego states. He further believes that psychoanalysis was not designed to deal with structural deficits, pointing out that Freud clearly indicated that analytic neutrality meant not promoting or gratifying infantile aims and wishes. Nevertheless, Blum wonders whether the psychoanalytic situation itself is a "holding," facilitating environment which, given the analyst's special qualities of empathy and acceptance, would remobilize developmental tendencies within the patient without the necessity of interpreting unconscious conflict. Blum concludes, however, that while important, the affective aspects of the analytic process are not a substitute for understanding and interpretation.

From the classical viewpoint, it is usually the changes in superego attitude that are considered the outcome of the corrective emotional experience. As mentioned in chapter 1, Freud wrote: "The new superego now has the opportunity for a sort of after-education of the neurotic. It can correct mistakes for which his parents were responsible in educating him." Freud was aware of the importance of the educative function of treatment. He wrote: "We cannot avoid taking some patients for treatment who are so helpless and incapable of ordinary life that for them one has to combine analytic with educative influence, and even with the majority, occasions now and then arise in which the physician is bound to take up the position of teacher and mentor." Surely this quotation suggests that Freud had a corrective emotional experience in mind for certain categories of patients.

Otto Kernberg has taken the position that the more severe the patient's ego distortion, the more it becomes necessary to replace a position of technical neutrality with the analyst's availability as an empathic, warm human being who permits the patient to internalize him and thus compensate for an arrested or incomplete early mother-child dyad. Kernberg, therefore, would reserve the "corrective emotional experience" for the severely disturbed patient. Kernberg adds that empathy is a necessary tool in every analyst's armamentarium, regardless of theoretical persuasion.

Kleinians do not address themselves to the question of the corrective emotional experience. They tend to hold the infant and his primitive, oral greed, and destructive impulses responsible for the fantasized image he has of his mother; moreover, they believe it is important to confront the patient with his split-off destructive impulses if the analysis is to be effective. Hannah Segal, however, has described projective identification as the earliest form of empathy, and views it as based on the capacity to put oneself into another's shoes.

Empathy in the self-psychological schema plays a far more significant and central role than in the classical analytic theory. To quote Kohut (1977) "the essence of psychoanalysis is that aspect of the world that is defined by the introspective stance of the observer." Wallerstein recognized the centrality of the concept when he stated: "Certainly all will agree on the powerful corrective emphasis that Kohut has given to empathy and introspection as central vehicles of the psychoanalytic endeavor." Wallerstein further points out that Kohutians have redefined empathy in terms of self-psychology.

Kohut has specified that the narcissistically disordered individual has not had adequate empathic mothering in his early developmental years, and so Kohut has devised certain variations of technique in order to provide that kind of experience for his patients. In this sense, a Kohutian analysis can be considered a corrective emotional experience. Arnold Goldberg (2007, p. 289) described Kohut's use of empathy as follows: "he connected to the patient by way of a temporary identification of a sharing of beliefs and feelings. This connection became elaborated into the psychological construction called the self-object in patients who in turn experienced the analyst as part of the self."

Those who subscribe to different analytic theories of therapeutic action would all agree that they meet with a patient's resistance to change—that is a given in analytic work. I am reminded of a story my former analyst told me while I was on the couch. I believe it was his attempt to point out the difficulties in working through conflicts in order to alter psychic structures and ultimately behavioral patterns. This is the story. A man was walking in a meadow on a bright, sunny day when he came across a deep, dark, black hole with snakes crawling around in it. He looked inside the hole and, to his surprise, he saw a man living in there. "Come out, come out!!" he exclaimed. "It's beautiful up here. Look at the purple hills, the crimson flowers, the green leafed trees!" The man peered out; he agreed that it was beautiful, calming, and inviting, but then he descended back into the hole, sliding the manhole cover back in place. There he knew who he was and how to adapt to the only world he had known. The fear of losing the relationship with early internalized objects has crystallized the now automatized defensive patterns of thought and behavior. It even has solidified the self-image or ego identity, so that letting go of neurotic behavioral patterns in the working through process becomes an arduous and prolonged undertaking. The fable I related is told from the object relations point of view; however, one could not only interpret the man's relations with the snakes as internalized self and object representations but as the accrued methodology in dealing with dangerous instinctual impulses and the anxiety they provoke, which might also be symbolized by the snakes. I think that my analyst wanted to point out to me that one can become trapped in a neurotic pattern. The psychic hole provides some kind of familiar comfort zone, despite its painful side effects. A therapeutic action can sometimes be difficult to effect in analysis; the resistance to change can be quite powerful.

It is difficult to present a uniform definition of therapeutic action that would be accepted by the various current analytic perspectives. To quote Michels (2007): "Psychoanalysis is not a defined method of therapy, but rather a number of different therapies . . . that share a history, many concepts and ideas and a community of discourses. However, they do not share a uniformity of method, agreement on what is essential and what is peripheral, or a theory of therapeutic action (p. 1725)." Kleinians hold to the idea that the agent of change is the interpretation of transference. Renik proposes that the relationship between the patient and the analyst is a collaborative one, and that insight is a co-construction. While Kohut, the creator of self psychology, believed that interpretation was important, it was more important that the analyst provide a positive substitute for the poor parenting experience the patient had as a child.

In the earlier history of psychoanalysis, therapeutic action was more easily defined. Following a classical line of thought, it promoted insight as the primary therapeutic action of psychoanalytic treatment. As Michel (2007) points out, the emphasis was placed on the pain of early relationships and the fantasies about them as well as the defenses erected to protect the patient from the pain of those early experiences. Loewald (1960) added to the theory of therapeutic action when he introduced the idea that the analyst's role in his relationship with the patient is like the mother of a child, emphasizing the importance of the parenting aspect of the patient's relationship with the analyst. So gradually the focus shifted to the significance of the patient-analyst relationship. Michel cites the problems involved in this shift (2007, p. 1730): "The therapeutic effect of the relationship was nonspecific—that is, it occurred in many other therapies, not only in psychoanalysis, and to some extent it even seemed anti-psychoanalytic, a concern that could hearken back to early discussions of 'suggestion' and 'transference cures.' The way in which psychoanalysis combines insight and relationship, along with those ways in which it understands and employs that relationship, that are distinctive from its use in other psychotherapies, became central concerns of the theory of psychoanalytic technique." The significance of that relationship, and possibly the form that it takes, varies in psychoanalytic treatment depending on the theoretical orientation of the analyst.

According to Turbin's description of relational technique, Relationists are flexible; they can borrow from the broad span of theoretical perspectives in psychoanalysis. They also can switch theories, depending on the nature of the problems the patient brings into the analytic session. They are not required to adhere to any specific therapeutic action rule; they can change their approach to the patient as long as the analyst continues to be warm and empathic. Stephen Mitchell described the Relational approach to treatment (1988, p. 3): "Relational-model theories view mind as fundamentally dyadic and interactive; above all else, mind seeks contact, engagement with other minds. Psychic organization and structures are built from the patterns which shape those interactions." Although Self Psychology is not always categorized as a relational theory, it also has emphasized the importance of being attuned empathically.

Owen Renik, an advocate of the relational approach, emphasizes, as his treatment goal, the patient's satisfaction and feeling of greater well-being. He points out that patients seek treatment because "they want to feel more satisfaction and less distress in their lives" (2007, p. 1547). At the same time, according to Turbin, Renik preserves a good deal of the traditional postulates of classical theory and technique.

In his chapter on Lacan, Romulo Lander (2007) describes Jacques Lacan's goal in psychoanalytic treatment as the patient's discovery of his "internal truth . . . there is no imposition of meaning or values, no intention of suggestion, and no demand for adaptation" (p. 1500). Those who followed Lacan's teachings called themselves Lacanians. Lacan viewed himself as Freudian. He was quoted as saying "It is up to you to be Lacanians, if you wish. I am a Freudian." He introduced the concept of *jousissance*, which had a central role in his theoretical conceptualizations. Lander described its function (p. 1507): "The necessary amount of *jousissance* that each subject needs in order to maintain his mental balance depends . . . on his infantile history. It is something embedded in his psychic structure and is thus part of that structure. It is not something that can be removed. It is something authentic to each subject, and each person has to learn how to live with it." It would seem that this concept is part of Lacan's form of therapeutic action.

Current psychoanalytic theories of therapeutic action all stress the important contribution of the patient-analyst relationship in effecting positive therapeutic action. Some stress the importance of interpretation and insight; however, before there can be a sound scientific foundation for the usefulness of the concept of therapeutic action, well-designed control studies are required to test and verify its relevance for psychoanalysis, and that would include using patients as subjects as well as analysts. I am aware, of course, that it is very difficult to design and implement such a study because of the variety of current psychoanalytic theories. First, the different theoretical analytic groups would each have to conduct their own study of therapeutic action among their members, followed by a comparative study of the different theoretical groups being studied.

I would like to state in closing that I certainly believe that it is important for the analyst to be warm and empathic in his relationship with a patient. I would not be successful in helping children or adults with their emotional problems if they did not perceive me in this way. But I do not believe that is the way they work out their emotional problems I believe that they improve because they gain insight into the underlying causes of these problems.

References

Abend, S. M. (2007). Essays on therapeutic action. *Psychoanalytic Quarterly* 76: 1413–416.

Abend, S. M. (2007). Therapeutic action in modern conflict theory. *The Psychoanalytic Quarterly* 76S: 1417–442.

Adler, K. (1980). Depression and suicide as theory related to intimacy and communication. *Modern Psychoanalysis* 5: 167–76.

Aisenstein, M. (2007). On therapeutic action. *Psychoanalytic Quarterly* LXXVI: 1443–62.

Alexander, F. (1950). Analysis of the therapeutic factors in psychoanalytic treatment. *Psychoanalytic Quarterly* 19(3): 482–500.

Allison, G. H. (1994). On the homogenization of psychoanalysis and psychoanalytic psychotherapy. A review of some of the issues. *Journal of the American Psychoanalytic Association* 42: 341–62.

American Psychiatric Association (1987). *Diagnostic and Statistical Manual of Mental Disorders*, 3rd ed. rev. (DSM-III-R). Washington, DC: American Psychiatric Press. Pp. 33–39.

Arlow, J. (1995). Stilted listening: Psychoanalysis as discourse. *Psychoanalytic Quarterly* 64: 215–33.

Baldwin, S. and Cooper, P. (2000). How should ADHD be treated? *Psychologist* 13(12): 598–602.

Barish, K. (2004). What is therapeutic in child therapy? Therapeutic engagement. *Psychoanalytic Psychology*, 21: 385–491.

Bartak, L. (1973). Special educational treatment of autistic children: A comparative study. Follow-up findings and implications for services. *Journal of Child Psychology & Psychiatry & Allied Disciplines* 14: 241–70.

Baruch, G. (1997). The impact of parental intervention on the analysis of a 5-year-old boy: A clinical approach. *International Journal of Psychoanalysis* 78: 913–26.

Beattie, H. J. (2004). Revenge. *Journal of the American Psychoanalytic Association* 53(3): 513–24.

Bemporad, J. R., Ratey, J. J. and O'Driscoll, G. Autism and emotion: An ethological theory. *American Journal of Orthopsychiatry* 57: 477–83.

Blatt, S. J. (1987). Internalization, separation, individuation, and the nature of therapeutic action. *The International Journal of Psychoanalysis* 28: 291–307.

Blatt, S. J. and Behrends, R. S. (1987). Internalization, separation-individuation, and the nature of therapeutic action. *International Journal of Psychoanalysis* 68: 279–97.

Blum, H. (1979). The curative and creative aspects of insight. *Journal of the American Psychoanalytic Association* 27S: 41–70.

Blum, H. (2011). Reflections on the past as prologue. *Journal of the American Psychoanalytic Association* 59: 11–26.

Blum, H. P. (1979). The role of identification of the resolution of trauma: The Anna Freud Memorial Lecture. *Psychoanalytic Quarterly* 56: 609–27.

Blum, H. P. (1981). Some current and recurrent problems of psychoanalytic technique. *Journal of the American Psychoanalytic Association* 29: 47–68.

Blum, H. P. (1997). Clinical and developmental dimensions of hate. *Journal of the American Psychoanalytic Association* 45: 359–75.

Blum, H. P. (2005). Psychoanalytic reconstruction and reintegration. *Psychoanalytic Study of the Child* 60: 295–311.

Boesky, D. (1983). The problems of mental representation in self and object theory. *Psychoanalytic Quarterly* 52: pp. 564–83.

Boesky, D. (1990). The psychoanalytic process and its components. *Psychoanalytic Quarterly* 59: 550–84.

Bowlby, J. (1960). Grief and mourning in infancy and early childhood. *The Psychoanalytic Study of the Child* 15: 9–52.

Brazelton, T. B. (1982). Joint regulation of neonate-parent behavior. In *Social Interchange in Infancy: Affect, Cognition, and Communication,* ed. E. Z. Tronic. Baltimore, MD: University Park Press. Pp. 7–22.

Breggin, P. R. (2000). A critical analysis of the NIMH multi-modal treatment study for attention/hyperactivity disorder. www.NIMH.nih.gov/publicat/adhdment.efm.

Brenner, C. (1982). *The Mind in Conflict.* New York: International University Press.

Brenner, C. (2008). Aspects of psychoanalytic theory: Drives, defense, and the pleasure-unpleasure principle. *Psychoanalytic Quarterly* 77: 707–17.

Brody, S. and Siegel, M. (1992). *The Evolution of Character: Birth to 16 Years.* New York: International University Press.

Brown, R. T. and Ievers, C. E. (1999). Psychotherapy and pharmacotherapy treatment outcome research in pediatric population. *Journal of Clinical Psychology in Medical Settings* 6(1): 63–99.

Burns, E. E, Fischer, S., Jackson, J. L., Harding, H. G. (2012). Deficits in emotion regulation mediate the relationship between childhood abuse and later eating disorder symptoms. *Child Abuse and Neglect* 36(1): 32–9.

Call, J. (1984). Child abuse and neglect in infancy. Sources of hostility within the patient-infant dyad and disorders of attachment in infancy. *Child Abuse and Neglect* 8(2): 185–202.

Carey, W. B. (2002). Is attention deficit a valid disorder? In *Attention Deficit: State of the Sciences, Best Practice.* Kingston, NJ: CRI Publishers. Pp. 1–17 (chapter 3).

Cipkala, G. (1998). Diagnosis and treatment of ADHD. *Perspectives in Psychiatric Care* 34(4): 18–25.

Cohen, K., Johnson, W., and Caparulo, B. (1976). Pica and elevated blood lead level in autistic and atypical children. *American Journal of Diseases of Children* 130: 47–48.

Colby, K. M. (1973). The rationale for computer-based treatment of language difficulties in nonspeaking autistic children. *Journal of Autism and Childhood Schizophrenia* 3: 254–60.

Cox, A., Rutter, M., Newman, M., and Bartak, L. (1975). A comparative study of infantile autism and specific developmental receptive language disorder: Part II, parental characteristics. *British Journal of Psychiatry* 126: 146–59.

Eissler, K. R. (1950). Ego-psychological implications of the psychoanalytic treatment. *Psychoanalytic Study of the Child* 5: 97–121.

Eizirik, C. L. (2007). On the therapeutic action of psychoanalysis. *Psychoanalytic Quarterly* 76: 1463–478.

Faimburg, H. (2005). *The Telescoping of Generations.* London: Routledge.

Fenichel, O. (1928). The clinical aspect of the need for punishment. *The International Journal of Psychoanalysis* 9: 47–70.

Fenichel, O. (1941). *Problems of Psychoanalytic Technique.* New York: Psychoanalytic Quarterly.

Fenichel, O. (1945). *The Psychoanalytic Theory of Neurosis.* New York: Norton.

Fiedler, F. (1950). A comparison of therapeutic relationships in psychoanalytic, nondirective, and Adlerian therapy. *Journal of Consult. Psychol.* 14: 436–45.

Fine, E. (2004). *ADHD: Rush to Judgment*. Unpublished paper presented October 2004 at the New Center for Psychoanalysis in Los Angeles.

Fine, S. and Fine, E. (1990). Four psychoanalytic perspectives: A study of differences in interpretive interventions. *Journal of the American Psychoanalytic Association* 38: 1017–48.

Fonagy, P. and Target, M. (1994). The efficacy of psychoanalysis for children with disruptive disorders. *Journal of the American Academy of Child Adolescent Psychiatry* 33(1): 45–55.

Frattaroli, E. (2001). *Healing the Soul in the Age of the Brain: Becoming Conscious in an Unconscious World.* New York: Viking.

Freud, A. (1928). The importance of earliest object relations. *The Psychoanalytic Treatment of Children.* New York: CRI Publishers, 1955.

Freud, A. (1936). *The Ego of the Mechanisms of Defense.* New York. International University Press. 1946, 1966.

Freud, A. (1965). *Normality and Pathology in Childhood.* New York: International University Press.

Freud, S. (1905). Three essays on the theory of sexuality. In *The Standard Edition of the Complete Psychological Works of Sigmund Freud,* Vol. 8.

Freud, S. (1914). On Narcissism. Standard Edition. In *The Standard Edition of the Complete Psychological Works of Sigmund Freud,* Vol. 14.

Freud, S. (1915). Observation on Transference Love. In *The Standard Edition of the Complete Psychological Works of Sigmund Freud,* Vol. 121.

Freud, S. (1919). Lines of advance in psychoanalytic therapy. In *The Standard Edition of the Complete Psychological Works of Sigmund Freud,* Vol. 17. London: Hogarth Press. Pp. 157–68.

Freud, S. (1923). The Ego and the Id. In *The Standard Edition of the Complete Psychological Works of Sigmund Freud,* p. 23.

Freud, S. (1926). Inhibitions, Symptoms and Anxiety. In *The Standard Edition of the Complete Psychological Works of Sigmund Freud,* Vol. 20: 77–175.

Freud, S. (1949). An Outline of Psychoanalysis. In *The Standard Edition of the Complete Psychological Works of Sigmund Freud,* Vol. 14.

Gabbard, G. O. (1994). Counter-transference: The emerging common ground. *International Journal of Psychoanalysis* 76: 475–85.

Glover, E. (1955). *The Technique of Psychoanalysis.* New York: International University Press.

Goldberg, A. (1974). On the prognosis and treatment of narcissism. *Journal of American Psychoanalysis Association* 22: 243–54.

Goldberg, A. (2007). Pity the poor pluralist. *Psychoanalytic Quarterly* 76: 1663–74.

Goldberg, J. G. (2004). Fantasies of revenge: Vengefulness and the stabilization of the ego: Acts of revenge and the ascension of thanatos. *Modern Psychoanalysis* 25: 3-21.

Greenson, R. (1967). *The Technique and Practice of Psychoanalysis.* New York: International University Press.

Greenson, R. R. (1954). The struggle against identification. *Journal of the American Psychoanalytic Association* 2: 200–17.

Greenson, R. R. (1965). The working alliance and the transference neurosis. *Psychoanalytic Quarterly* 34: 155–81.

Hanley, C. (1994). Clinical advantages and disadvantages of multiple models. *Psychoanalytic Inquiry* 14: 164–84.

Hartmann, H. (1939). *Ego Psychology and the Problem of Adaptation.* New York: International University Press, 1958.

Hartmann, H., Kris, E., and Lowenstein, R. M. (1946). Comments on the formations of psychic structure. *The Psychoanalytic Study of the Child* 2: 11–38.

Hartmann, H., Kris, E., and Lowenstein, R. M. (1949). Notes on the theory of aggression. *The Psychoanalytic Study of the Child* 3: 9–36.

Hobson, R. P. (1983). The autistic child's recognition of age-related features of people, animals, things. *British Journal of Developmental Psychology* 1: 343–52.

Hobson, R. P. (1990). On psychoanalytic approaches to autism. *American Journal of Psychiatry* 60: 324–36.

Horney, K. (1948). The value of vindictiveness. *American Journal of Psychoanalysis* 8: 3–12.
Indersitzin, L. B. and Levy, S. T. (1994). On grist for the mill: External reality as defense. *Journal of the American Psychoanalytic Association* 42: 763–87.
Jones, J. D. (2002). Plea for a measure of understanding the importance of intensive psychotherapy: The treatment of children with ADHD. *Psychotherapy: Research/Practice/Training* 39(1): 12–20.
Kanner, L. (1944). Early infantile autism. *Journal of Pediatrics* 25: 211–17.
Kanner, L. (1943). Autistic disturbances of affective contact. *Nervous Child* 2: 217–50.
Kernberg, O. F. (1955a). On identification. In *New Directions in Psychoanalysis*. New York: Basic Books, 309–45.
Kernberg, O. F. (1955b). Notes on countertransference. *Journal of the American Psychoanalytic Association* 13: 38–56.
Kernberg, O. F. (1957). *Envy and Gratitude*. New York: Basic Books.
Kernberg, O. F. (1969). A contribution to the ego-psychological critique of the Kleinian School. *International Journal of Psychoanalysis* 50: 317–33.
Kernberg, O. F. (1974). Contrasting viewpoints regarding the nature and psychoanalytic treatment of narcissistic personality: A preliminary communication. *Journal of American Psychoanal. Association* 22: 255–67.
Kernberg, O. F. (1975). *Borderline Conditions and Pathological Narcissism*. New York: Aronson.
Kernberg, O. F. (1979). Some implication of object relations theory for psychoanalytic technique. *Journal of the American Psychoanalytic Association* 50, pp. 317–33.
Kernberg, O. F. (1982). Self, ego, affects, and drives. *Journal of the American Psychoanalytic Association* (suppl.), pp. 207–40.
Kernberg, O. F. (1984). *Object Relations Theory and Clinical Psychoanalysis*. New York: Aronson.
Kernberg, O. F. (1986). Identification and its vicissitudes as observed in psychosis. *International Journal of Psychoanalysis* 67: 147–59.
Kernberg, O. F. (1987). Projection and projective identification: Developmental and clinical aAspects. *Journal of the American Psychoanalytic Association* 35: 795–820.
Kernberg, O. F. (1996). The analyst's authority in psychoanalytic situation. *Psychoanalytic Quarterly* 65: 137–57.
Kernberg, O. F. (2007). The therapeutic action of psychoanalysis: Controversies and challenges. *Psychoanalytic Quarterly* 76: 1689–724.
Klein, M. (1946). Notes on some schizoid mechanisms. *International Journal of Psychoanalysis* 27: 110.
Klein, M. (1955). On identification. In *New Directions in Psychoanalysis*. New York: Basic Books, pp. 309–45.
Klein, M. (1957). *Envy and Gratitude*, New York, Basic Books.
Klein, Melanie. (1950). *The Psychoanalysis of Children*. London: The Hogarth Press Ltd. Pp. 11–13.
Klein, Melanie. (1952). On observing the behavior of young infants. *Developments in Psychoanalysis*, London: The Hogarth Press Ltd. Pp. 237–70.
Klein, Melanie. (1952). *Some Theoretical Conclusions Regarding the Emotional Life of the Infant*, London: The Hogarth Press Ltd. Pp. 198–236.
Klein, Melanie. (1952). The emotional life of the infant. In *Developments in Psychoanalysis*, London: The Hogarth Press Ltd. Pp. 198–236.
Knight, Rona. (2005). The process of attachment and autonomy in latency. A longitudinal study of ten children. *Psychoanalytic Study of the Child* 60: 178–210.
Kohut, H. (1971). *The Analysis of the Self.* New York: International University Press.
Kohut, H. (1977). Reflections on the occasion of Jean Piaget's eightieth birthday. *The Annual of Psychoanalysis* 5: 373–75.
Kohut, H. (1977). *The Restoration of the Self.* New York: International University Press.
Kohut, H. (1978a). *The Search for the Self,* 2 vols., ed. P. Ornstein. New York: International University Press.

Kohut, H. (1978). The disorders of the self and their treatment: An outline. *International Journal of Psychological Analysis* 59: 413–25.
Kohut, H. (1979). The two analyses of Mr. Z. *International Journal of Psychoanal.* 60: 3–27.
Kohut, H. (1977). The oedipus complex and the psychology of the self. *The Restoration of the Self*, pp. 220–48.
Kohut, H. (1984). *How Does Analysis Cure?* Chicago: Chicago University Press.
Kris, E. (1950). Preconscious mental processes. *Psychoanalytic Quarterly* 19: 540–60.
LaFarge, L. (2006). The wish for revenge. *Psychoanalytic Quarterly* 75: 447–75.
Lakin, M. and B. Liebovitz. (1978). Bias in psychotherapists of different orientations: An exploratory study. In *The Scientific Evaluation of Freud's Theories and Therapy*, ed. S. Fisher and R. P. Greenberg. New York: Basic Books. Pp. 390–96.
Lander, R. (2007). The mechanisms of cure in psychoanalysis. *Psychoanalytic Quarterly* 76: 1499–512.
Lane, R. C. (1995). The revenge motive: A developmental perspective on the life cycle and the treatment process. *Psychoanalytic Review* 92: 41–64.
Leichsenning, F. (1965). Are psychodynamic and psychoanalytic therapies effective? A review of empirical data. *International Journal of Psychoanalysis* 86: 841–68.
Leichsenning, F., J. Biskup, R. Kreische, and H. Staads. (2005). The Gottingen study of psychoanalytic therapy. First results. *International Journal of Psychoanalysis* 86: 433–55.
Livingston, R. (1987). Sexually and physically abused children. *Journal of the American Academy of Child and Adolescent Psychiatry* 26(3): 413–15.
Loewald, H. W. (1960). On the therapeutic action of psycho-analysis. *International Journal of Psychoanalysis* 41: 16–33.
Loewald, H. W. (1971). The transference neurosis: Comments on the concept and the phenomenon. *Journal of the American Psychoanalytic Association* 19: 54–66.
Lussier, A. (1991). The search for common ground: A critique. *International Journal of Psychoanalysis* 72: 57–62.
Mahler, M. S. (1968). *On Human Symbiosis and the Vicissitudes of Individuation*. New York: International University Press.
Mahler, M. S. (1979). *The Selected Papers of Margaret S. Mahler*, Vol. 1. New York: Jason Aronson.
Mahler, M. S. (1963). Thoughts about development and individuation. *Psychoanalytic Study of the Child* 42: 307–24.
Menninger, K. (1993). Love against hate. *Psychoanalytic Review* 30: 47–475.
Michels, R. (2007). The theory of therapeutic action. *Psychoanalytic Quarterly* 76: 1725–734.
Mitchell, S. A. (1988). *Relational Concepts in Psychoanalysis*. New York: Harvard University Press. Pp. 1–40.
Modell, A. (1994). Common ground or divided ground. *Psychoanalytic Inquiry* 14: 201–11.
Oas, P. T. (2001). *Curing ADD/ADHD*. Raleigh, NC: Pentland Press, Inc., 201.
Olds, D. D. (2006). Interdisciplinary studies and our practice. *Journal of the American Psychoanalytic Association* 54: 857–75.
Ornstein, A. (1997). A developmental perspective on the sense of power, self-esteem, and destructive aggression. *The Annual of Psychoanalysis* 25: 145–54.
Paniaqua, C. (1995). Common ground, uncommon methods. *International Journal of Psychoanalysis* 72: 57–62.
Pine, F. (1988). Four psychologies of psychoanalysis and their place in clinical work. *Journal of the American Psychoanalytic Association* 36: 571–96.
Pine, F. (2011). Beyond pluralism: Psychoanalysis and the workings of mind. *Psychoanalytic Quarterly* 80: 823–56.
Pozzi, M. (2002). Ritalin for whom? Understanding the need for ritalin in psychodynamic counseling with families of children under five. *Journal of Child Psychotherapy* 26: 25–43.
Pulver, S. E. (1987). How theory shapes technique: Perspectives on a clinical study. *Psychoanal. Inq.* 7: 141–299.
Rapaport, D. (1951). The conceptual model of psychoanalysis. *Journal of Personal.* 20: 56–81.
Reed, G. S. (1987). Rules of clinical understanding in classical psychoanalysis and in self psychology: A comparison. *Journal of American Psychoanal. Association* 35: 421–46.

Renik, O. (2007). Intersubjectivity, therapeutic action, and analytic technique. *Psychoanalytic Quarterly* 76: 1547–562.

Ritvo, E. R., and Freeman, B. J. (1984). A medical model of autism. *Pediatric Annals* 13: 298–305.

Ritvo, E. R., Ornitz, E. M., and La Franchi, S. (1968). Frequency of repetitive behavior in early infantile autism and its variants. *General Psychiatry* 19: 291–347.

Ritvo, E. R., Yuwiler, A., Geller, E., Kales, A., Rashkis, S., Schieor, A., Plotkin, S., Axelrod, R., and Howard, C. (1971). Effects of L-dopa in autism. *Journal of Autism and Childhood Schizophrenia* 1: 190–205.

Rosen, L. C. (2005). Revenge—The hate that does not speak its name: A psychoanalytic perspective. *Journal of the American Psychoanalytic Association* 55.

Rosenblitt, D. (1996). States of overstimulation in early childhood. *The Psychoanalytic Study of the Child* 51: 542–61.

Rosenblitt, D. L. (2005). Translating child analysis from the playroom to the classroom: Opportunities and choices. *Journal of the American Psychoanalytic Association* 53: 189–238.

Rothstein, A. (1998). Neuropsychological dysfunction and psychological conflict. *Psychoanalytic Quarterly* 67: 218–39.

Rutter, M. (1966). Behavioral and cognitive characteristics of a series of psychotic children. In *Early Childhood Autism*, ed. J. K. Wing. Oxford: Pergamon Press, 51–81.

Rutter, M. (1967). Psychotic disorders in early childhood. In *Recent Developments in Schizophrenia*, eds. A. Coppen and A. Walk. *British Journal of Psychiatry*, Special Publication no. 1, 133–158.

Rutter, M. (1968). Concepts of autism: A review of research. *Journal of Child Psychology and Psychiatry* 9: 1–25.

Rutter, M. (1970). Autistic children: Infancy to adulthood. *Seminars in Psychiatry* 2: 435–50.

Rutter, M. (1973). The assessment and treatment of preschool autistic children. *Early Child Development and Care* 3: 13–29.

Rutter, M. (1974). The development of infantile autism. *Psychological Medicine* 4: 147–63.

Rutter, M. 1972). Childhood schizophrenia reconsidered. *Journal of Autism and Childhood Schizophrenia* 2: 315–37.

Rutter, M., (1968). Concepts of autism: A review of research. *Journal of Child Psychology & Psychiatry* 9: 1.

Sacks, O. (2003). The mind's eye. *The New Yorker* 27(20): 48.

Salomonsson, B. (2006). The impact of words on children with ADHD and DAMP: Consequences for psychoanalytic technique. *The International Journal of Psychoanalysis* 87: 1029–47.

Sanchez-Cardenas, M. (2011). Matte Blanco's thought and epistomological pluralism. *International Journal of Psychoanalysis* 92(4): 811–31.

Sandler, J. (1990). On internal object relations. *Journal of the American Psychoanalytic Association* 38: 859–79.

Sands, S. H. (1997). Self psychology and projective identification—whither shall they meet? *Psychoanalytic Dialogues* 7: 651–68.

Schain, R., and F. Freedman. (1961). Studies of 5-hydroxyindole metabolism in autistic and other mentally retarded children. *Journal of Pediatrics* 58: 315–20.

Segal, B. (1996). The Role of Pathological Self Objects in the Development of a Form of Defensive Self. *Psychoanalytic Quarterly* 75: 747–59.

Segal, H. (1963). *Introduction to the Work of Melanie Klein*. New York: Basic Books.

Segal, H. (1977). Psychoanalytic dialogue: Kleinian theory today. *Journal of the American Psychoanalytic Association* 25: 363–70.

Shafi, M. (1979). Childhood psychosis. In *Psychosis of Childhood*, Vol. 2, ed. J. D. Noshpitz. New York: Basic Books, 555–67.

Shedler, Jonathan. (2010). The efficacy of psychodynamic psychotherapy. *American Psychologist* 45(2): 89-100.

Shengold, L. (1985). The effects of child abuse as seen in adults: George Orwall. *Psychoanalytic Quarterly* 54: 20–45.

Sherkow, Susan P. (2011). The dyadic psychoanalytic treatment of a toddler with autism spectrum Q disorder. *Psychoanalytic Inquiry* 31: 252–75.
Silverman, Martin A. (1982). The latency period: Early female development. In *Current Psychoanalytic Views*, ed. K. Mendell. Pp. 203–26.
Solnit, A. J. and J. Call. (1979). Psychosexual development five to ten years. *Basic Handbook of Child Psychiatry*, Vol. I, 186–90.
Spezzano, C. (2007). A home for the mind. *Psychoanalytic Quarterly* 76: 1563–583.
Spillius, E. B. (1988). *Melanie Klein Today: Developments in Theory and Practice*, Vol. 2. London: Routledge.
Spillus, E. B. (1992). Clinical experiences of projective identification. In *Clinical Lectures: Klein and Bion*. New York: Routledge. Pp. 59–73.
Steele, B. (1983). The effect of abuse and neglect on psychological development. In *Frontiers of Infant Psychiatry*, ed. J. Call, E. Galenson, and R. Tyson. New York: Basic Books.
Steele, B. (1994). Psychoanalysis and the maltreatment of children. *Journal of the American Psychoanalytic Association* 42: 1001–25.
Stern, D. (1985). *The Interpersonal World of the Infant: A View From Psychoanalysis and Developmental Psychology*. New York: Basic Books.
Stolorow, R., and Lachmann, R. (1980). *The Psychoanalysis of Developmental Arrests*. New York: International University Press.
Strachey James. (1969). The nature of the therapeutic action of psychoanalysis. *The International Journal of Psychoanalysis* 50: 275–92.
Sugarman, A. (2006). Attention deficit hyperactivity disorder and trauma. *The International Journal of Psychoanalysis* 87: 237–41.
Sussenwein, F. (1971). A developmental and behavioral approach to the treatment of preschool autistic children. *Journal of Autism and Childhood Schizophrenia* 1: 376–97.
Trevarthen, C., and P. Hubley. (1978). Secondary intersubjectivity: Confidence, confiding, and acts of meaning in the first year. In *Action, Gesture, and Symbol: The Emergence of Language*, ed. A. Lock. London: Academic Press. Pp. 183–230.
Tustin, F. (1981). *Autistic States in Children*. London: Routledge and Kegan Paul.
Tustin, F. (1991). Revised understanding of psychogenic autism. *International Journal of Psycho-Analysis* 72: 585–91.
Wallerstein, R. S. (1985). How does self psychology differ in practice? *International Journal of Psychoanalysis* 66: 391–404.
Wallerstein, R. S. (1986). Letter to the editor. *International Journal of Psychoanalysis* 67: 505–506.
Wallerstein, R. S. (1988). One psychoanalysis or many? *International Journal of Psychoanalysis* 69: 5–21.
Wallerstein, R. S. (1990). Psychoanalysis: The common ground. *International Journal of Psychoanalysis* 71: 3–19.
Wallerstein, R. S. (1995). The relation of theory to technique. *Journal of Clinical Psychoanalysis* 4(4): 527–42.
Walters, A. S., Barrett, R. P., and Feinstein, C. B. (1990). Social relatedness and autism: Current research, issues, directions. *Research in Developmental Disabilities* 11: 303–26.
Weil, A. P. (1970). The basic core. *The Psychoanalytic Study of the Child* 25: 442–60.
Weinshel, E. M. (1990). Some observations on the psychoanalytic process. *Psychoanalytic Quarterly* 3: 63–69.
Weinshel, E. M. S. (1990). Further observations on the analytic process. *Psychoanalytic Quarterly* 59: 629–49.
Widener, A. (1998). Beyond ritalin: The Importance of therapeutic work with parents and children diagnosed ADHD. *Journal of Child Psychotherapy* 33(1): 45–55.
Wright, J. L. (2006). Psychoanalysis in conjunction with medication: A clinical research opportunity. *Journal of the American Psychoanalytic Association* 54: 833–55.
Yorke, C. (1994). Freud or Klein? Conflict or compromise? *International Journal of Psychoanalysis* 75: 366–75.
Zetzel, E. R. (1969). The technique and practice of psychoanalysis. *International Journal of Psychoanalysis* 50: 411–12.

Index

About the Author

Dr. **Esther Fine** has been a practicing psychotherapist for the past sixty years. She brings her psychoanalytic knowledge and expertise to the treatment of both adults and children.

www.ingramcontent.com/pod-product-compliance
Ingram Content Group UK Ltd.
Pitfield, Milton Keynes, MK11 3LW, UK
UKHW020905190926
475560UK00010B/220

9 780765 709493